Ticket to Minehead

TAUNTON TO MINEHEAD BRANCH

MINEHEAD
DUNSTER
BLUE ANCHOR
WASHFORD
WATCHET
WILLITON
STOGUMBER
CROWCOMBE
BISHOPS LYDEARD
BARNSTAPLE
NORTON FITZWARREN
TAUNTON
EXETER
LONDON

Ticket to Minehead

Alan Hammond, Christine Hammond & Richard Derry

Millstream Books

This book is dedicated to
Bert Blake
who passed away on 4 February 2004

In 1976, after retirement, Bert joined the West Somerset Railway as a volunteer. He later became a guard and then stationmaster at Minehead. Bert was a gentleman and loved his railways, especially the WSR where he gave many years of loyal service. You could not wish to meet a nicer man and those who were lucky enough to come into contact with him will always remember that cheery smile and his genuine love and help for others. We feel privileged to have met him and he will never be forgotten by us or by the many members of the West Somerset Railway.
(Photograph by courtesy of Kay Cheesman)

Cover illustrations:
(front) An interlude in time at Williton station in 1961. Fireman John Fisher and the signalman chat with the passengers, while the porter makes sure everybody is on board. The train is hauled by a class 5700 No.8745 with a morning stopper to Taunton. (Gerald T. Robinson)
(back) On a warm, sunny day, with North Hill in the background, Prairie Tank No.4143 awaits departure from Minehead with a Taunton-bound train. (R.E. Toop)

First published in 2005 by
Millstream Books, 18 The Tyning, Bath BA2 6AL

Set in Times New Roman and printed in Great Britain by
The Amadeus Press, Cleckheaton, West Yorkshire

© Alan Hammond, Christine Hammond and Richard Derry 2005

ISBN 0 948975 73 3

British Library Cataloguing-in-Publication Data:
a catalogue record for this book is available from the British Library

Foreword

My earliest railway memories are of exploring the derelict Victorian goods shed at my home town railway station in Gloucestershire. Amidst the eerie solitude I would spend hours trying to imagine the bustling atmosphere of steam at this busy Cotswold town; shunted goods wagons and the screaming whistle of the passenger express on the close-by main line. Not having the real thing I had to be content with the simulated puffing noises of the electric toy train set that circulated the bedroom. I'm not too sure that it used real coal to achieve this effect. But I do recall carrying coal from our bunker to put in my goods wagons, spreading coal dust everywhere as I did so, and that my bedroom door only ever opened about a foot for years. This pleased my parents greatly! But at least they knew that I was happy.

As far as reality was concerned I still enjoyed the smell of diesel and the chugging DMUs (diesel multiple units) that passed through Stroud station. I can still feel the cold of a late Sunday evening in winter, as the regular weekly stop of a Class 47 pulled the Paddington express from Gloucester. I did collect engine numbers for a while, and it didn't seem to matter that it was the same engine every week! I was still fascinated for those magical few minutes.

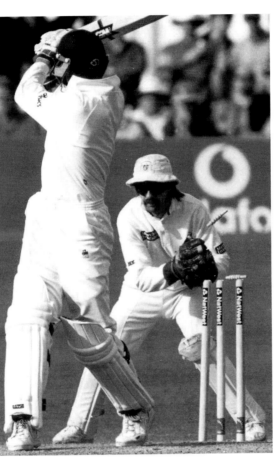

Just one of Jack Russell's 128 stumpings in a 23-year first-class career which included 54 test appearances for England.

At times I wish I had been born into a different era. If I had seen the steam system in the flesh, I am sure I would have become an artist much earlier in my life. I would have craved to record its wonderful living atmosphere on canvas. However it was a very wet few days during a cricket match at Worcester, where Gloucestershire were playing Worcestershire in a county championship game, when the unrelenting rain had stopped play, that I discovered a glimmer of the artist hiding inside. Fed up with the inactivity I walked into the town and purchased a small sketch book and some pencils. On my return journey I noticed a man sitting under a tree reading a newspaper, and began to draw. The result encouraged me to pursue a second career as an artist. Now I have my own art gallery in the High Street in Chipping Sodbury just north of Bristol.

So I was delighted to discover the West Somerset Railway. The first train I ever painted in the 'flesh' was on a very wet and windy November day at Minehead Station. I was made very welcome by the station staff. But the sea breeze was so strong I had to employ most of them to stop my easel, canvas, palette and brushes flying off the platform and onto the track. The painting was bought by my good friend Terry Bowden who, together with Mike Hitchens, was responsible for introducing me to the West Somerset Railway. I also bumped into an old friend of mine from my early cricketing days, Ron Ireland, who was driving engines on the line, and passing on his vast knowledge to the many enthusiasts. Having retired from playing professional cricket, I will make a real effort to spend much more of my time painting on the West Somerset Railway. Also, if I ask nicely, more rides on the footplate with my old pal Ron. Can't wait!!!

So enjoy Alan, Christine and Richard's *Ticket To Minehead* which brings back the memories of a golden era on this railway.

Jack Russell
2005

Introduction and Acknowledgments

We all live in Minehead and have written quite a few railway books between us. On many occasions we have been asked: 'Why don't you write a book about people's memories on the old Taunton to Minehead branch'. Well, we have taken up the challenge and we hope you enjoy *Ticket To Minehead*. We have tried to give as many different memories of the railway as possible from the 1920s to closure in 1971. We have interviewed staff, passengers, enthusiasts, holidaymakers, evacuees and people travelling to and from work and school. The stories are mostly railway driven, but we have also added insights into the lives of contributors, which includes many local characters who were part of the community in Somerset. We have also added a number of photographs at the Taunton end of the line to show the different motive power that came into that station and an account of a trip to Paddington by a 16-year-old fireman, who has given us interesting stories of trips on other nearby branches as well.

What is so rewarding about doing a book like this, is that the railway from Bishops Lydeard to Minehead lives on, thanks to a great many people who over the years have built up the West Somerset Railway into one of the premier preservation railways in the country.

Like all books of this nature, many people have contributed in different ways. Special thanks go to Jack Russell for writing the foreword and to Tim Graham, our publisher, for his support, design skills and faith in our project. A really big thank-you must go to John Simms of the West Somerset Railway, our one-man publicity guru. Melvyn Baker has been a great help in tracking down names for the staff photos in the book, as has David Woolford. Also our grateful thanks to John Pearce who has been a real help in allowing us to go through his photograph collection, as have Peter Triggs, Walter Harris, Trevor Martin, Ben Norman, Peter Lock, Peter Lockwood, Margaret Gould, Iris Horn and many others.

Our sincere thanks go to all the contributors of the memories and photographs in the book. Special mention must go to our proof readers Allan Stanistreet, Dr. James Thomas, Irene Hammond, Frances Bristow, Melvyn Baker, Roy Pitman, Pam & Graham Hooper, Gillies Watson, Will Widden and Stuart Newsham.

Many others have given us great assistance in many ways and our thanks go to West Somerset Railway, *West Somerset Railway Journal*, Mark Smith, Mike Chilcott, Audrey Holcombe, Tim King, Ern Dingle, Alan Grieve, Alan Porton, Michael Hodge, Chris Dyer, Sid Dunscombe, Brian Harding, Dave Johnson, Josephine Sheppard, Paul Conibeare, Roy Phippen, Alfie Littlefield, David Grimmett, Jan Stevens, George Reeder, Harry Kirkland, Roy Hobbs, Chris Sheppard, Brian Winter, Steve Martin, Ben Norman, Daphne Case, Reg Webber, Peter Treharne, Roy Cross, John Cockrem, the late Leon Kidson, Stan White, Richard Beel, John Harris, Ken Hill, Ron Heywood, Joanne Woolford, Peter Clements, Christopher van den Arend, Hetty Heard, John Cornelius, Vera Bradshaw, Kay Cheesman, Ruth Bulpin, Margaret Snell, Harold Gibbs, Julia Jones, Violet Crawford, Winnie Earl, Grahame Page, Fred Hutchings, Jean Grandfield, Sue Illingworth-Kay, Ron White, Donald Amies, Mike Haynes, Alan Scott, David Williams, Richard de Jong, Graham Stagg, Gordon Harris, Colleen Baker, Judy Hall, Barbara Burdge, David Welch, Mike Hitchens, Jim Ruston, Don Harris and Jack Binding.

As many photographs are from personal collections and have no attribution, a reader may well recognize a photograph that he or she took. In this case we offer our apologies in advance for not being able to credit you in person.

Alan and Richard would like to offer special thanks to Christine. She has been a tremendous help with her keyboard skills and efforts in spending many hours cleaning and repairing the photographs.

The authors, photographed in the 1970s when the Minehead branch closed. From left to right: Richard Derry, Christine Hammond and Alan Hammond.

Short History of the Branch

The branch as far as Watchet was designed by Isambard Kingdom Brunel in his last years, before he died in 1859. The same year, work started on the building of the line which ran from a junction at Norton Fitzwarren on the Bristol-Exeter main line near Taunton. A station was not opened here until 1873 although the branch to Barnstaple was opened in 1871.

The original Bristol-Exeter line had been built to the broad gauge which arrived at Taunton in 1842 and reached Exeter by 1844. Work on the first part of the branch went as far as the port of Watchet and the line was built to the broad gauge and opened in 1862. During 1876 the main lines through Taunton were adapted to mixed gauge so that trains could also run on the standard gauge. Evidence that Watchet was once the terminus of the line is shown by the main building on the station being sited at right angles to the track; it is still in use by the present West Somerset Railway. Stations on the Watchet branch were built at Bishops Lydeard, Crowcombe, Stogumber, Williton and Watchet with a level crossing provided at Williton. Only Crowcombe did not have a goods shed.

In 1870 the Minehead Railway Company obtained an Act of Parliament to extend the branch from Watchet up to Washford and down to the sea with stations at Blue Anchor, Dunster and terminating at Minehead. This part of the branch was opened in 1874 and the train service was operated by the Bristol and Exeter Railway. Train services over the Norton Fitzwarren to Watchet section were also supplied by the Bristol and Exeter Railway but the Watchet to Minehead section still remained an independent company. Although the B&ER was absorbed by the Great Western Railway in 1876, the latter did not take over the Minehead branch until 1897. This led to the GWR operating the line on behalf of the WSR board until the grouping of the railways when it all became part of the GWR and the line was now the Minehead branch.

The line could not continue to operate to the broad gauge and the branch was converted to the standard gauge in 1882. From the start the main traffic was passengers, remaining fairly consistent, with a peak in the 1930s when ten stopping trains per weekday were regular on the branch. Through trains to and from Paddington were common occurrences, though not always calling at all stations on the branch.

There were no major mineral deposits in the area except for what was being carried on the West Somerset Mineral Line, unlike that across the water where South Wales was built on coal. Local companies sent their produce along the branch, paper to and from Wansborough Paper Mill at Watchet, as well as agricultural products, wool and livestock. Coal of course came down the line, especially for the steam locomotives that hauled all the trains on the branch. Watchet Docks was once a source for goods such as the esparto grass, imported via the docks.

At first the branch was run on the time interval system which basically required accurate timekeeping and no locomotive failures. The year 1868 saw the electric telegraph introduced to the line. By 1876 interlocked points and signals were in operation and the GWR in 1895 had its own pattern of electric train staff. This was updated in the twentieth century. Increased traffic in the 1930s saw the GWR improve the line by the introduction of Leigh Bridge Loop between Crowcombe and Stogumber stations and Kentsford Loop between Watchet and Washford. The Dunster to Minehead track was doubled. These changes added greater flexibility to the branch.

Under the terms of the Transport Act of 1947, nearly all railway lines in the United Kingdom were nationalized in 1948. The GWR was now history; the Minehead branch was owned by British Railways and came under the control of the Western Region. Gradually cutbacks were introduced to the line when staff numbers were reduced, and stationmasters ran more than one station. Some stations became un-staffed. One publication quotes station manning levels from over 50 in 1938 to 11 in 1970. Goods traffic was reduced and general goods facilities were withdrawn in 1964. The biggest change in the 1960s was the replacement of steam locomotion by diesel locos on goods trains and diesel multiple units on the passenger services. Eventually the branch closed to all traffic in 1971.

BRISTOL AND EXETER RAILWAY

Opening of the West Somerset Railway

TAUNTON to WATCHET

On Monday, 31st March, this line will be opened for

PASSENGER TRAFFIC

and the following trains will run:—

DOWN TRAINS

LEAVING			Class 1 & 2	Class 1, 2 & 3	Class 1 & 2	Class 1, 2 & 3
			a.m.	p.m.	p.m.	p.m.
Taunton	.	.	9.50	2. 5	5.00	7.30
Bishops Lydeard	.	.	10.5	2.19	5.14	7.44
Crowcombe Heathfield	.		10.19	2.33	5.28	7.58
Stogumber	.	.	10.26	2.40	5.35	8. 5
Williton	.	.	10.35	2.49	5.44	8.20
Watchet (arrival)	.	.	10.40	2.55	5.50	8.20

UP TRAINS

Watchet	.	.	8.45	12.30	3.30	6.15
Williton	.	.	8.52	12.36	3.36	6.21
Stogumber	.	.	9. 5	12.49	3.49	6.34
Crowcombe Heathfield	.		9.12	12.56	3.56	6.41
Bishops Lydeard	.	.	9.22	1. 5	4. 5	6.50
Taunton (arrival)	.	.	9.35	1.18	4.18	7. 3

This line will open a direct Route to LYNTON, PORLOCK, MINEHEAD etc., and well regulated coaches will run from Williton in connection with the Expresses and Third Class Trains.

by order of the Directors,

HENRY DYKES,

Superintendent.

Bristol, 19th March, 1862.

(Reproduced from an original owned by Mr. J.H. Horn, formerly stationmaster at Stogumber)

A bird's eye view of Minehead taken from North Hill. The date stamped on the back of this postcard is 1910, but when was the photograph actually taken? (*West Somerset Steam Railway Trust collection*)

David Woolford

Well, there we were, my mother, brother and myself standing on the platform at Taunton station waiting for the train to Minehead. It was early spring in 1955, and we were moving to Minehead in order to be near to my mother's family. We boarded the train, and little did I know at that time that I would soon be working on the line and that I would later marry the young lady sitting opposite me in that train compartment. I was nearly 15, and it was my original intention to continue my education in Minehead, but on visiting the local school I found the syllabus was very different to my previous school. Against better advice I decided to seek employment in Minehead until I was called up for National Service which was still compulsory at that time. On visiting the local employment exchange, I was offered the position of booking clerk at Minehead station. This bore no relation to what I really wanted to do but I thought the position would be a suitable stopgap. I attended an interview with the then stationmaster, Tom Stewart, who was rugby mad. Within a few days I sat an entrance exam which was held at Taunton station and shortly afterwards my application for employment was confirmed. At the age of 15 my life on the line began.

On my first day at work I presented myself at Tom Stewart's office and he took me on a brief tour of the station and introduced me to various members of staff including the chief clerk Percy Harris and parcels clerk Mervyn Berryman. Percy was a dapper man, who often sported a buttonhole. He loved his cricket, read *The Financial Times*, and was affectionately known as Cocker. Percy and Mervyn set about teaching me the ticket issue system, how to read the timetables, and the other daily, weekly and monthly routines.

One of the things which amused me on my first day at the station was the entrance system to the booking office. In order to maintain security, any member of staff wishing to enter the office would give a secret knock and the door would then be opened by means of a cord which was attached to the door latch and then threaded through a series of pulleys around the office. This meant that without leaving your position of work it was possible to open the door simply by pulling the cord. I do not know who dreamt up this system, but it worked very well, and made life easier at busy times.

Although I still felt like a raw novice, Percy decided I knew enough of the basics to work unsupervised. Within a few short weeks I found myself working single-handed early and late shifts in the booking office. The shift system suited me down to the ground as it fitted in nicely with my passion for fishing.

Each day in the booking office we had to balance the cash taken with tickets issued, and we always balanced to the penny. Once a day the cash was bagged up and then despatched by train in the safe in the guard's van. There was a fair amount of daily, weekly and monthly paperwork to deal with, including postal requests for tickets, seat reservations and enquiries. All of this became second nature and although we were kept busy we were only stretched during the summer months.

The highlight of each morning was when Jack Davis the ticket collector came round to collect the pie order. He would then cycle up The Avenue to Venn's Deli, shortly to return with the cooked pies. We would then gather round the pot-bellied stove in the parcels office to relish the pies, washed down with station tea, sweetened with condensed milk. We would read the free newspapers salvaged from the down trains. To this day I have never found any pies to equal Humphrey Venn's, and it is no wonder my weight shot up to over 17 stones while I was working on the line.

When on the late shift, together with porter Sam Cornish, I would often sample the roast beef sandwiches from the Beach Hotel. I can remember grilling local herrings, which had just been caught, in front of the booking office stove. Now and again we received consignments of live chickens in baskets, and more often than not we would find eggs. Some members of staff had allotments on railway land, and when a plot became available I took one on. My plot was sited right in front of the Station Terrace houses, and quite near to the turntable. This site is now covered in tarmac, and forms part of the car park.

Reading a railway timetable soon became second nature to me. As many enquiries were for the same destination, quite often I did not have to refer to the timetables at all, as the information was ingrained. However, one enquiry, soon after I started single-handed shifts, sticks in my mind. I was about to finish the late shift, when a person came to the booking office window and asked me to write down the times for a service to Criccieth. Minehead to Criccieth was a booking clerk's nightmare, but in the end I did manage to come up with the required information; I locked the office a bit late that night. The next morning I asked Percy Harris to check the details I had given, and luckily for me all was well. However, I later found out that I had been set up by a certain member of staff who was not my favourite person for a while.

During the summer months the station was very busy, especially on Saturday with the through trains. On Mondays the booking hall would be heaving with passengers wishing to make seat reservations for their return journeys on the following Saturday. We would open a second window in the booking office just to deal with the mass of seat reservations, the queues seemed to be never-ending. It was very important not to make mistakes with seat reservations as a double booking caused chaos when two families turned up to claim the same seats, with no spare seats available. Thank goodness such incidents were very few and far between. The porters were always ready to assist passengers with their luggage as this usually resulted in a tip. I can remember working during a strike by NUR members (the salaried staff elected not to strike), there was nothing for us to do as there were no trains. I was very sympathetic to the uniformed staff, as I often wondered how they managed to raise their families on such low wages.

In the winter months life was much more leisurely, and between trains Percy Harris loved to relate to me his experiences during the war, and between us we would put the world to rights.

When Mervyn Berryman moved away from Minehead, I took over as parcels clerk, but still did some early and late shifts in the booking office. I soon settled into the new routine, dealing with such things as passenger luggage in advance, lost property, left luggage and consignments of all shapes and sizes into and out of Minehead, including arranging collections and deliveries. There was usually some fun when a horse box was being loaded, for some reason the horses seemed to hate leaving Minehead. I recall working a shift in the booking office on Christmas Day, one train in and one out. In return for this, there was the attraction of days off in lieu and enhanced pay.

When the position of stationmaster was phased out at Dunster station, a leading porter Donald Spencer became general factotum, but a member of the clerical staff at Minehead had to visit Dunster at regular intervals to audit the ticket-issue book and other items. I used to enjoy this job and would travel up by train to check the books. If it was a fine day I would often walk back to Minehead along the track, sometimes munching a Russet apple scrumped from the tree in Dunster station grounds and hoping to find some mushrooms on the way.

One day there was a robbery at Dunster station when a youth broke into the office and stole various tickets and other items. I was called upon to check all ticket stocks and to list all the missing items. The local Police soon caught the culprit and I had to attend court as a witness to confirm the items stolen and their value. When I calculated the value of the missing items, I used the actual train fares as the basis of my calculation. However, it was pointed out to me by the court that as the tickets had not been date stamped they were only worth the paper and printing costs. This made no difference to the outcome, as the youth was found guilty.

All members of staff were encouraged to take a railway examination each year and I always took part in this. There was a postal course followed by an examination at Exeter. This meant that those members of staff taking part travelled to Exeter to sit the exam. It was on one such occasion that I first sampled the delights of a raw onion sandwich washed down with cold beer at *The Red Cow* in Exeter.

Another of my duties was to prepare the rota for the taxi rank, and to collect the taxi rents from the proprietors who used the station rank. Matters were arranged so that each taxi owner took his turn at being first on rank, which in theory gave the first on rank a better chance of obtaining a fare. However the system often worked in favour of the second or even third on rank, as the first passenger requiring a taxi may have only required a trip to Alcombe, whereas the second passenger might have been heading for Porlock or Lynmouth, resulting in a much higher fare. I do not know if the story is true but I heard that one passenger asked for a taxi to the Beach Hotel, not realising it was just across the station yard, only to be taken on a trip round the town before being delivered back to the Beach.

When Butlin's came to Minehead, we did notice an increase in rail traffic, and a small office was opened within the camp; this was staffed by Ron Heywood and one porter.

Although the station ran like clockwork most of the time, there were serious problems from time to time. One train ran into a herd of cows, which had somehow got on to the line. I can remember the white-faced members of staff talking about bits of cow everywhere. On one occasion a blind man alighted from the wrong side of the train in Minehead and fell to the ground instead of stepping onto the platform he assumed was there. On another occasion a young girl had her hand crushed when a carriage door was slammed shut on it. Then there was the time a train driver became distracted and hit the buffers in Minehead at quite a speed causing some damage. The branch line was very nearly extended out to sea. Another incident I will never forget was when a local person blew a whistle and waved a flag and sent a passenger train on its way to Taunton, whilst the guard was still drinking tea in the parcels office. The guard had to take a taxi to Dunster where he took control of the train once more.

The Beatles train was another event which caused a stir and I can remember the screaming girls at the station railings. I was on the platform alongside the train with other members of staff, but as far as I can remember none of us managed to speak to the Fab Four.

Jack Davis the ticket collector always tried to hold a train if a regular passenger was a bit late. One such day a lady passenger was running across the station yard, when Jack noticed she had dropped something. Jack told her to board the train and said he would retrieve the lost item. Jack then went to pick up the item only to find it was a sanitary towel, red faces all round. Another time Jack and I were walking across the station yard to our allotments, when we both saw a £1 note on the ground. We bent down at the same time and there was a clash of heads; I cannot remember what happened to that £1 note.

In 1964 I left the railway and married the young lady who had been sitting opposite me on the Minehead train. National Service was phased out just before I was due to be called up, so my stopgap job lasted for much longer than I expected. There are many other members of staff I remember with affection; most of them are now travelling that long branch line in the sky. I am still in touch with one or two, and whenever we meet we always talk about our days on the line. Some 41 years after I worked on the line I look at the thumb nail on my right hand and I can still see the ridge caused by the date stamp in Minehead booking office.

(*left*) Porter Gordon Meade on the approach road to Minehead goods shed in the 1950s. He spent most of his working life on the railway. The building on the left was the old bungalow café. (*Margaret Snell collection*)

(*above*) Station staff and footplate crew join together for a team photograph at Minehead station. From left to right: porter Donald Spencer, stationmaster Ernest Rose, guard Reg Bending (who used to carry his own teapot around with him), driver Tom Phillips and fireman Des Hartnell. (*Jean Grandfield collection*)

(*right*) Leading porter Percy Howe stands proudly at Minehead station. Look at the travel bargains of 27/- to Plymouth and 18/6d. to Bristol. How times have changed. (*Julia Jones collection*)

Four Ladies

Hetty Heard, Vera Bradshaw (*née* Reed), Violet Crawford, Winnie Earl

These four wonderful ladies worked on the GWR at Minehead station during the Second World War and it was thanks to Hetty Heard that she got all the ladies together for a trip down memory lane. Sadly they don't remember the dates they started as it was 60 years ago and it had been a long time since they'd been asked to think so deeply about these times.

Vera: (*Booking office*) In between booking tickets we had great fun, we'd tell tales of what we did the night before. During the day Mr. Smallridge the chief booking clerk would get on our backs about work, but we would still have a good giggle between us.

Hetty: (*Booking office*) Chief booking clerk Charles Smallridge was very tall and every morning he would pull himself up to his full height and in a deep voice say 'Good morning ladies'. He was extremely good as a boss and a very nice man, also Tom Stewart the stationmaster was a perfect gent. I remember getting £2.12s a week and we were paid less than the men. We had a 07.00 start with the first up train at 07.30 and worked until 14.00 on one shift or 15.00 to 22.00 on the other or until the last train came in which could be at any time. Normally due in at 22.30, it often arrived after midnight especially if London had been bombed. This caused big delays and meant the last branch train would have to be held for the last London train. No overtime would be paid and often there were only two or three passengers getting off the last train.

Winnie: (*Porteress*) We had to unload the parcels from the guards van on the last train and one night there was a corpse on the train. Whoever she was we left her there overnight as she wasn't going anywhere. Monday-Saturday was normally worked with sometimes the odd Sunday, though Saturday was from 07.00 to 19.00, which of course meant a 12-hour shift. It was a very busy day with trains in both sides of the station and often a queue all the way along the yard for the London train.

Violet: (*Porteress*) The Yanks trained on North Hill and brought their tanks in on rail transporters. They would unload them in the goods yard and drive them through the town and up to North Hill. At one time the tanks came to Minehead when they should have stopped at Norton Fitzwarren. One day I was taking a delivery of fish up to the guards van, which came from Mac Fisheries and was a local delivery to Blue Anchor. In the guard's van was one Yank in charge of army staff. He said to me 'Would you like to give me a kiss'. I ran down the platform as fast as I could go.

Hetty (*having been shown a staff photograph of ten people*): Oh yes that's Mr. Luxton, he worked on the goods side, he was a very brave man, he lost both his legs in the First World War. He used to come to work in a battery carriage. Roy Hobbs was senior on the goods side, Bill Greenslade was one of the firemen and Mr. Moody one of the drivers. Oh, it all comes back to you after a while. We walked or cycled to work. I used a sit-up-and-beg bike, which the Yanks found amusing when I rode it into work. I even got a lift in on a coal lorry one winter's morning when it was snowing.

Violet: Canadians and Americans were stationed at Dunster and would walk the line from Minehead to Dunster if they missed the last train, or they couldn't or wouldn't pay the fare. This was stopped because of their drinking as they couldn't handle the local cider. In a drunken state, what would have happened if they'd met a train on the line? One day some officers came down and one said 'We want to walk the line'. I said 'Oh no you don't'. 'We want to walk the line', they demanded. Well, I replied: 'No one is allowed to walk the line and that also means you'. They turned around and walked out. The Avenue Hotel in Glenmore Road saw Yanks staying there and parading at 07.00. When walking to work I would be asked to 'turn round' and also I received plenty of wolf whistles. I got fed up with this, so I used another route to get to work, often the little lane near the Beach Hotel.

Hetty: At 07.00 a lot of soldiers would be preparing to travel so I would issue a bulk travel ticket for a group of them. Sometimes at the end of the day after we had locked up the station Mr. Stewart would say 'Come on girls, you've worked hard all day' and he would take us all over to the Beach Hotel for a drink at his expense. A train came in once and guard Fred Chidgey was banging on the pub window and he said 'I think, ladies, you'd better come over and let everybody out'. All the gates were locked and passengers were trying to climb over the fence and gates.

(*above*) Station staff at Minehead in the 1950s. From left to right, top: Percy Hobbs (guard), Fred Coles (carter) and Sam Cornish (porter); bottom: Charles Smallridge (chief booking clerk), Ena Stevens (porteress), Tom Stewart (stationmaster), Winnie Earl (porteress) and Jack Davis (ticket collector). (*Steve Martin collection*)

Hetty and Violet: We pooled our food, which was rationed because of the war, which included baked beans, bacon and eggs. We had basic cooking facilities on the station; sometimes the footplate crews gave us a fry up on the firing shovel.

All: We found no resentment from the men, we were all treated as equals, they were very nice and sensible and would help us if required. They did the heavy work especially with the horseboxes.

Winnie: On one of the last trains there was a cow in a horsebox and it calved on the way down to Minehead. However, it was lame and the horsebox was shunted into a siding to be dealt with the next day. I'm not sure if we charged excess for the extra passenger.

All: Fred (Lofty) Coles was very tall, he ran a horse and dray to deliver luggage around Minehead. Harry Sparks drove the lorry, he lived at Dunster and the two guards were Fred Chidgey and Sam Case.

Violet and Hetty: Ada Bartlett was one of two ladies who worked in the signalbox along with Dan Dinwiddy who was a bit of a lad. The box was then situated on the north side of the running lines and a lot of open land could be seen from the box. Ada once phoned up: 'Come and see what this couple are doing in the grass'. This went on all the time on this open land especially when the soldiers were stationed in the area.

Violet: Two Yanks asked Ada when she was in the box: 'If we come up will you show us how to turn them points'. Ada replied: 'Be off or I'll come and turn your points'. A lot of the Yanks got ruined by cider and once when checking their tickets one said he'd got on at Dunster but he didn't have a ticket. The fireman told me that the soldier and his mate had got on at Watchet. 'No we didn't, we got on at Dunster, not at Watchet' he said, so I told them: 'Right, excess fare' and I got the book out. 'You old so and so, you ought to be out amongst the Germans'. I told him: 'I've got a husband and brother fighting for the likes of you'. So I sloshed him right across the head and knocked his hat flying.

15

Winnie and Violet: Harry Sparks, who drove the delivery van, cycled into work and we often used to decorate his bike and even tied it to the ceiling. It took him ages to get it down. One day we helped get some parcels out of the van but he locked us in, drove us up to North Hill and made us walk back.

Hetty: Wages got paid on a Friday. The men would line up half an hour before they were given out. Mr. Stewart paid it out but I'm not sure how he made them up or whether they were delivered by train. The ordinary fare to Taunton was 1/11d single and 3/6d return; staff travelling got 75% off the fare.

Winnie and Vera: The Bacon train saw a return fare of 1/6d and ran late in the afternoon and was so named as it ran to Taunton where people would purchase their groceries. Food was cheap. We often bought the Sunday joint and caught the last train back. It ran in the 1930s and we often got back at midnight.

Hetty: The Strand Café was great for doughnuts, which we had for our break, they were specially made. At night when the Gaiety Theatre had a function on, us girls would go over for a dance.

Violet: In town was Boddies the Bakers where we also got food. I once used a bike left in the cloakroom to cycle up town to get the cakes, but when I got back on it again I'd taken the wrong bike.

All: One day Jack Davis who was the ticket collector and Violet were working in the left luggage office. They were not making many tips, so he took his cap off and wrote a thank-you note to place in it. At the end of the day they shared out the tips. They often made a good amount of money on the platform. Jack would also walk along with a false limp when he was carrying luggage to earn sympathy from the passengers and get more tips.

Pigeons were sent by rail and often when Jack Davis was weighing in the pigeon basket, either end would be held by the owners so less weight was recorded, so there would be less to pay. They would be sent to Williton to be released, then on to Bishops Lydeard, Taunton and then Highbridge. They would go further down the line when they became more experienced. The time released would be filled out on a card and returned with the empty baskets.

Vera: Food could be obtained from the Marshes, like ducks, pheasants, rabbits and even fish to help supplement the food for the evacuees. We shared everything. One family called Fitzgerald had 11 mouths to feed and local kids never went without. One of the ladies who came down from Worcester felt she was far better fed down here than in the Midlands. People who worked on the land got a cheese ration and a good supply of vegetables.

Winnie: One of my neighbours wondered why he didn't get a bacon ration; well his wife was selling the ration, so she could purchase cigarettes. On early turn I used to take the station teapot over to the Beach Hotel where the cook would put hot water in the pot for me and if it was cold she would put a tot of whisky in it. Happy Days.

Violet: Fred Chidgey, one of the guards, came into the place where we had a fire one day and took his hat off and threw it down; he was as bald as could be. I said to him 'Come here a minute'. I kissed him on top of the head and it left a lipstick mark. When I saw him again he said: 'You so and so'. 'What's wrong?' I said. 'My wife nearly put in for a divorce, she thought I was seeing somebody else'.

Vera: When the evacuees went back at the end of the war I saw one away who had stayed with us; it was like saying goodbye to a sister that day on the station; there were tears in my eyes. I went back to my mother and we broke our hearts. We still write to each other at Christmas; she now lives near Taunton.

Violet: I preferred wearing the issue skirts to the trousers which we could also wear. My husband cleaned my GWR buttons for me. There was one porteress at Watchet who was too large for her trousers, she used an elastic band to keep them up. Well one day I crept up behind her and with a pair of scissors cut the elastic band. You can imagine the result.

Hetty: In the booking office you had to check every train revenue to the last penny; if it didn't balance you had to do it all again. I also had to make out weekly and monthly proofs. One woman I worked with was quite useless with figures and it was always me looking for that elusive penny. Mr. Smallridge would go right through the figures and it had to jolly well balance. He'd stand there by the counter and sharpen pencils to a long point and became aggravated if a pencil point broke off. Every train, arrival or departure, he had to sharpen that pencil.

Winnie: Jack Davis had to light any straw he found on the platform; wherever it was, he had to put a light to it. One time in the left luggage office he set the fire going, but the chimney had not been swept and it caught fire. You couldn't see across the road because of the smoke; people in Porlock thought Minehead station was on fire.

A father and son were evacuated from London; on one train the son was into everything in the guard's van and he emerged waving a green flag. The train pulled away and left the guard on the platform with the driver thinking he had got the right of way. The train was held at Dunster and the guard was taken there by taxi. After that, the young evacuee was not allowed anywhere near the station.

Jimmy Doble, a steam raiser, lived in Station Terrace. He would come over to the station last thing at night to build up the fire in the engine which was stabled in the single road engine shed. He would do this after the last train had come in; he would use the turntable, bank the fire up in the engine and at 06.00 in the morning, make sure the fire was ready for the crew coming on at 07.00. A lot of evacuees came out of London on the last train, often with babes in their arms with little luggage and they'd sleep in the train all night. At 06.00 Jimmy would come along and turn them out and they would occupy the seafront, where the Strand Café would open at 06.30 to provide breakfast for them.

Hetty: The girls were a lovely crowd to work with, smashing people, but I had to move to Braintree, Essex, because my husband was in the RAF and was transferred there; it was called Doodlebug Alley. It was so different to the quiet of Somerset. In our lodgings we were shown a metal shelter downstairs. A few nights later I was woken by what I thought was a motorbike. I looked out of the window, it was a Vl rocket and I could see the exhaust of the engine. I've never moved so fast to get to that shelter. Since we've come back, I've spent many happy years living here in Minehead.

Hetty and Vera: We worked very well together. The 14.10 from Taunton on Saturdays was always busy. One day many people arrived on this train; there were kids in the luggage racks, like peas in a pod. Bed and Breakfast was 7/6d and all around the station were B&Bs, especially in Glenmore Road and Ponsford Road. Not all the kids were trained and many mattresses had to be thrown out. Of course they brought their ration books with them.

All: It is a long time ago now, but we are still all friends and even today we have a chuckle about the days on the branch.

GREAT WESTERN RAILWAY.

Telephone No.

...........................DEPARTMENT,
MINEHEAD. STATION,
2st. 11. 19.44.

Your reference :—

Please quote this reference :—

Mrs Heard, 8 Meadow Road, Alcombe, Minehead.

Mrs Heard has been employed at this station for the past eighteen months as a Booking Clerk, and has given every satisfaction.

I have always found her very conscientious, diligent, and trustworthy, and can confidently recommend her for any post involving reliance, dependability, and integrity.

It is with regret that I lose Mrs Heards services.

Mrs C. Stewart.
Stationmaster.

(*above*) The single road engine shed at Minehead opened in 1874 by the Bristol & Exeter Railway. It was a sub-shed to Taunton in GWR days and during BR days stayed the same, though Taunton had been recoded 83B. Closed in November 1956, the shed area is now covered in tarmac, though the buildings in the background still exist. (*R.K. Blencowe collection*)

(*below*) 2-6-2T No.4128 of Taunton shed at the head of what appears to be a summer Saturday through train. Note the fireman standing on the bunker looking towards the photographer. (*Walter Harris collection*)

(*above*) Minehead goods yard in 1964. Of interest are the crane, BMC Austin lorry and trailer, the loading gauge and the empty cattle pens. The station closed to goods on 6 July 1964. (*Michael Hodge*)

(*below*) With the Minehead station sign prominent, class 5700 No.3736, having left its train in the platform road, is now running round to carry out some shunting, before heading back up the branch. (*Colour Rail collection*)

Ron Heywood

I started at Minehead station as a junior clerk in the booking office in 1950. Colleagues I recall were stationmaster Tom Stewart, chief booking clerk Charles Smallridge, chief clerk in the goods office Mr. Hudson and parcels office clerk Percy Harris. Ron Davis and myself made up the staff in the booking office covering the early and late turns. The goods office clerks were George Luxton, Mervyn Berryman and another whose name I can't recall, plus a female clerk, who again I cannot remember, but she lived with her parents at Carhampton where her father was the local blacksmith. I believe their name was Hawkins. The ticket collector was Jack Davis, father of Ron in the booking office. Porters were Percy Howe, Sam Cornish and one other who divided their time between the parcels office and the platform. Goods delivery lorry drivers were Sam Case, Stan Dunscombe and Ern Crockford; the parcels lorry driver was Fred Coles. The shunter was Harry Sparks, who used to walk the back road from Dunster every morning to start shunting duties at 06.00, when the first goods train arrived, with the second goods train arriving at lunch time.

When Tom Stewart was there he was President of the Minehead Barbarians rugby team, in fact he practically ran it. On Friday afternoons you couldn't get into his office for all the rugby shirts from the previous game, drying and airing around the coal fire which used to get red hot.

When Charles Smallridge retired, Percy Harris became chief clerk. When Tom Stewart retired Ernest Rose became stationmaster (the last one at Minehead). In 1950 nearly all the stations had their stationmasters but as time went on they were gradually done away with, until Mr. Rose was the only one left; he looked after the rest. When Percy Harris died, Jim Neville, who had been the stationmaster at Dunster, took over the booking office at Minehead until the branch

A distinguished array of railwaymen at Minehead station, probably taken in the 1930s. From left to right, top row: Percy Howe? (porter), unknown, Len Palk (porter), Percy Hobbs (guard), Sam Case (guard), Tommy Kemp (signalman), Charlie Fullard (goods office), unknown, unknown. Middle row: Charles Smallridge (chief clerk), Percy Harris (parcels clerk), Mr. Morris (stationmaster), George Luxton (goods clerk), Mr. Connett (goods office). Bottom row: Arthur Case (carter), Jack Davis (ticket collector), unknown, unknown. (*Daphne Case collection*)

closed. The signalmen at Minehead were a Mr. Denny and one other, and latterly Harry Phippen who came from the Blue Anchor box. Ron May was the relief signalman and operated in all the boxes as necessary.

When Butlin's opened I used to run the railway office in the camp during the summer months and had a porter on Saturdays to help out with all the luggage. Percy Hobbs, who had been a guard on the branch, came out of retirement to do this.

The railway internal telephone system was such that each station had a code and whilst all the bell codes rang in every office you only answered to your code. Minehead booking office was five bells, then a pause, and then one bell. Mind you, you could pick up the phone any time and listen into other people's conversations. It also served a good purpose in that you were always warned by the staff on the branch when any VIP railwaymen were on the way.

The gangers, who were responsible for maintaining the track on the branch, were based at Minehead. One of the maintenance gang was Bill Storey who walked the line from Dunster to Blue Anchor every day checking the line. He would then catch a train from Blue Anchor to Minehead and then walk the line from Minehead to Dunster. Another ganger was Johnny Redfern, who had come down from Newcastle many years before and played football for Minehead.

The steam engines were operated by two sets of drivers and firemen, all based at Minehead. Jimmy Doble was the engine cleaner who worked nights and had to have the engine all prepared for the crew for the first train out in the morning. He lived in a cottage in Station Terrace and the engine shed was within yards of his home.

There were three horses for delivering goods. The stables were where the boxing club is now. The carters were Fred Coles, Gordon Meade and Harry Fitzgerald. Blacksmith Alan Arnold used to keep the horses shod. His employer Norman Case had to go down to the stables if there was a severe frost and put special frost nails in the shoes. It is hard to imagine that it was 55 years ago when I first started on the branch.

A photo of staff at Minehead on the retirement of a colleague. Top, from left to right: Robin Strong (junior clerk), Ernie Crockford (goods porter), Alfie Littlefield (goods porter), Sam Cornish (porter), Sam Case (guard) and Clarence Aylesbury (relief clerk). Bottom: Ernest Rose (stationmaster), George Luxton, the retiring goods clerk, with his toaster, Tom Stewart (retired stationmaster) and Ron Heywood (booking clerk). (*Ron Heywood collection*)

(*above*) It is 1951 and No.5327, then based at 82A Bristol Bath Road shed, is seen at Minehead at the head of a stopping passenger train. Note Café Strand on the right-hand side. (*Owen Mogg/Peter Triggs collection*)

(*left*) 2-6-0 No.6333 in platform 2 at Minehead in the 1950s, at the head of a short passenger train. The position of the man at the rear of the tender suggests he is about to couple the loco- motive to the train. (*Richard de Jong*)

(*above*) Arthur Case delivering goods on his GWR horse and cart, passing the Conway Hotel (now Winsor nursing home) in The Avenue, Minehead. His father, Sam Case, was a guard on the branch in the 1930s. (*Daphne Case collection*)

(*right*) Carter Stan Dunscombe, on the left, driving the GWR horse and cart outside the Beach Hotel, Minehead. Look at the lady's hat in the background, dating the photograph to the 1930s. (*Sid Dunscombe collection*)

Minehead loco shed in 1952. Class 4575 No.5533 is seen shunting some wagons whilst No.6373 waits on shed. (*R.J. Sellick/Williton Station collection*)

Peter Lockwood

In 1952, at the age of 15, I began the task of learning to be a motor mechanic at the Metropole Motor Garage in Minehead. My wages were £1. 10s per week. At my mother's insistence I attended Taunton Technical College one whole day per week. This was approximately 25 miles from my home at Golsoncott, near Roadwater. To get there I cycled two miles to Washford railway station and travelled the rest of the way by steam train. The fare to Taunton was 4/3d return. I would carry my bicycle up the steps and onto the platform and leave it against the outside wall of the ticket office. There was only one railway employee at Washford station if I remember correctly, and he gave out the little cardboard tickets and carried out all the other station duties on his own. There was an evening lesson, 18.00-20.00 at the college, and the last train from Taunton to Minehead left Taunton station at around 21.30 arriving at Washford at around 22.00.

I clearly remember the old sepia pictures of beauty spots and seaside resorts, four per compartment, above the seat backs. In the centre of the carriage wall was a pivoting lever to control the compartment heating. In cold weather we would move the lever to maximum heat, which would result in a hissing sound and perhaps some small amount of steam from under the seat, but never a great deal of warmth. I never re-member having to re-position the lever because we were too warm.

My father's health failed in 1957 and we left Golsoncott to live at Bratton, two miles outside Minehead. I now travelled the full length of the Minehead to Taunton line to complete my studies at Taunton Technical College. In 1961 I began a new course of day-release study at college, travelling once more by rail from Minehead station, but soon the steam engines were replaced by diesel multiple units. It was still an excellent service, reliable and, dare I say it, more comfortable. The smell of the smoke and the steam had gone. One could now open a window without particles of soot blowing in, but it had somehow become a more characterless form of travel. The slight feeling of achievement at reaching the end of a long journey by steam train had gone. Travel had become bland.

The railway engineers and apprentices that I studied with at college told me that the Minehead line was operating at a loss. At least I was able to complete my studies in 1964 while still travelling by rail. The journey from Minehead to Taunton by rail took 45 minutes but it took twice as long by omnibus and was only half as comfortable. It was impossible to write my homework during the journey.

Trains for Paddington Mondays to Saturdays Winter 1959...							
	a.m	a.m	a.m	p.m	p.m	p.m	p.m
Minehead depart	7-35	9-05	10-50	12-20	1-50	1-50	5-05
Taunton depart	9-35	10-40	12-05	1-35	3-05	4-15	6-25
Reading	—	12-42	2-06	4-49	—	6-25	—
Paddington arrive	12-15	1-25	2-50	5-35	6-10	7-15	9-0

Change at Taunton and Bristol. + Change at Taunton Only.

The winter timetable of 1959 on Minehead station was photographed by a member of staff.
The timings speak for themselves. (*David Woolford*)

One of the largest locomotives to run on British tracks was LMS 4-6-2 Pacific No.6229 *Duchess of Hamilton*. It is seen here on the turntable at Minehead, before going to Butlin's on static display, c.1964. (*John Pearce collection*)

Grahame Page

As part of a programme on the West Somerset Railway, a TV producer asked the railway volunteers why they worked on the railway. I replied 'Hitler' and the scene was not transmitted. The truth of the matter was that I happened to be one of several hundred kids evacuated from the London Blitz and again in 1943/44 when the V2s started raining down. My grandfather worked for the LNER at Stratford Works for most of his life and his father was employed by the Great Eastern, so steam was in my blood. Where we lived, N7 Tanks were the most visual motive power with an occasional F5 making an appearance.

So as an excited six-year-old you can imagine my reaction to seeing my first loco with a name, at the head of the evacuees' train from Paddington to Taunton, which was a Castle class No.5043 *Earl of Mount Edgecumbe*. I can still remember this clearly, even if more recent events have faded from my memory. We changed at Taunton and ended up at Blue Anchor, where we alighted. We were taken to what I suppose might have been army tents on the beach, our new home, where I could watch the trains at the level crossing for hours. I recall seeing another loco with a name *Chaffinch*, the only time I ever saw it on the branch, the other engines being mainly Prairies, Panniers and 2251s.

After some time we moved to a house in Minehead, which I hated, as it was some way from the station and I was only allowed an occasional treat. Here I recall Western National Bristol H buses and a Leyland coach with a fin on the roof at the back, which I now know is a dorsal fin Harrington-bodied Leyland Cheetah, operated by Scarlet Coaches or Blue Motors. After Minehead we were taken on a Devon General bus to Babbacombe near Torquay for a period of time and then back to London behind *King Henry III*, which took us all day and into the night because of air raids.

Then in 1944 it happened all over again and Minehead was again my temporary home, hence my affinity with the WSR. After all, steam is in my blood.

Other memories I recall were a 14-coach train from Minehead to Paddington with locos changing at Taunton. With no lights in carriages, you might stop somewhere in the countryside for no apparent reason, because of extra trains, probably troop move-ments, which had priority. I remember a bit of a flap when we were on the Blue Anchor beach camp, as a fighter had crashed further along the coast and it might have been near Minehead golf course. More recently, talking to a local man, he told me that General Eisenhower stabled his train on the branch before D-day; whether this is true I don't know.

Railways, in particular the West Somerset Railway, are still part of my life. I am an active volunteer since retiring and I have even bought a house called Puff Cottage.

From left to right, with the background of the Lido Olympic-sized Art Deco swimming pool at Minehead, are holidaymakers young Judy Hall (*née* Swainsbury), Albert Swainsbury and Christine Aldridge, c.1961. (*Judy Hall collection*)

A Taunton-bound train at Minehead in platform 2 at some time in the 1930s. The locomotive, although referred to as a member of the 4500 class, is one of the 4575 class introduced in 1927. One of the improvements was increased water capacity, and no doubt the engine was based at Taunton shed. (*R.K. Blencowe collection*)

Will Widden

My father and I witnessed the following incident one day in 1920 while waiting for a connection at Taunton station. We were en-route from Cardiff to Ilfracombe and had some time to wait for our train. My mother spent the time in the waiting room while dad and I walked up and down the platform. We noticed a tiny calf's head protruding from a sack which was tied to an upright post of the overhead bridge. Both having an interest in the GWR (dad as an employee), we were pleased to learn the world famous Cornish Riviera would be passing through before our stopper. As soon as the Riviera was sighted, a young porter ran towards the calf. He quickly untied the rope, picked the animal up in his arms and went outside to what is now the taxi rank and waited until the train had passed. Once it went through he retied the calf back to the post. As we joined our train we saw the same porter hand this animal to the guard. That incident has remained in my memory for 84 years – another good report for God's Wonderful Railway.

Twenty years later, another but very different incident happened on the down platform. In the course of my full-time employment as a trade union officer, I had an occasion to visit Ilfracombe, and again I had to change at Taunton. I joined the Barnstaple train waiting in the bay platform. I noticed the driver walking back along the platform peering into each compartment. As he approached my window I realised he was a long-standing friend who I had last heard of at Severn Tunnel Junction; he was now based in Taunton. We had time for a few minutes' chat.

Our use of the Minehead branch did not start until we had moved to London. Previously we had used P&A Campbell's White Funnel Fleet's magnificent steamers from Cardiff to Ilfracombe. The steamers were the easiest means of travelling from Cardiff to Ilfracombe during the season. In winter the GWR became a great way round as it meant changes at Bristol, Taunton and Barnstaple, there re-booking, as it was the London and South Western Railway for the final part of an exhausting journey. Later, to continue our long association with Minehead we used the Saturday morning through trains from Paddington and back.

My first journey by White Funnel was at the tender age of three months (so I have always been informed). Soon afterwards, the outbreak of war meant rail only until late 1919. The ship would often call at Minehead and I always liked the sweep of the bay though not the gasworks so near the pier. Little did I know the important part that this lovely town, as well as the White Funnel fleet, was to play in my life. In 2001 I bought a book on the history of the fleet at Ilfracombe Museum and flicking through the photographs I found one of myself landing at Ilfracombe in July 1928 on my way to work in one of the family's catering establishments.

The story now switches to two sisters in a Cardiff Bakery and confectionery business of which we were customers. On one bright Sunday the two girls decided to visit Ilfracombe for the first time. It was a choppy sea and whilst the elder girl proved a good sailor her sister was anything but. So when the ship stopped at Minehead, the two girls landed, intending to return by rail. As they walked along the quay they asked a lady in one of the cottages the way to the station, telling her the reason why. The lady, a Mrs. Brewer, told them to wait for the evening boat as the sea and wind would have gone down by then and they took her advice, which was totally correct. On the way to the pier, they called on Mrs. Brewer to thank her. The elder girl noticed a B&B sign on the wall of the cottage and asked if she could visit when she could get a weekend off, and so started a friendship of many years standing. On her first visit this young lady noticed a colour print of Widecombe Fair on the bedroom wall; this of course has in the chorus my surname. On the spur of the moment she remembered the railwayman's son and sent me a postcard. This led to our meeting regularly and in 1937, to a marriage which lasted 57 years. Interestingly when I was first invited to share weekend trips I had to sleep in a neighbour's house. What a difference to present-day morals.

When Mrs. Brewer died we would stay at *The Plume of Feathers* and on one holiday we took my mother-in-law with us. She was a very strict woman, little given to offering praise. It was a surprise to my wife and me when on the through train one Saturday morning before we reached Taunton, she said it had been a lovely holiday. The food at the hotel was excellent and the bed, the most comfortable she had ever slept in.

In 1985 we kept a promise we made to each other before we were married, that in retirement we would move to Minehead. We enjoyed several happy years together, but in the early '90s my wife's health began to fail and she died in 1994. My memories of Minehead will always be with me.

We hope the weather has not been bad for their Christmas holiday. They look well wrapped up as they board their train home. One of the passengers on the far right is Olive Pomroy. Look at the old-fashioned suitcases. (*Trevor Martin collection*)

Richard Beel

When World War I started in 1914 my father was a telegraph clerk in Taunton Post Office. He had married in 1910 and now had a baby daughter six months old. So it came as something of a surprise to find that he was to be seconded to the Coast Guard Service and to take up duties forthwith at their lookout post at Hurlestone Point, that jutting headland at the eastern end of Porlock Bay. What warlike actions were anticipated in this rather isolated region remain a World War I mystery. The nearby tiny village of Bossington did not even have a public house. However, even had there been a village pub, my father was a strict teetotaller. So father did the obvious thing and looked around the village for accommodation to bring his small family to Bossington. He succeeded in finding a second home with Mr. and Mrs. Will Floyd, thereby starting an association which was to last throughout their lives – and even beyond, as my sister, a great walker, continued to stay in the village until she could walk no longer in the mid 1980s – and I still call back at odd intervals.

This rather long introduction explains how the Beels came to Bossington and brings us to the time of my first journey as a small child on the Minehead line as we called it, which was probably round about 1925. By now a very firm friendship with the Floyds had developed and it had become customary to spend a week with them most years, either in the spring or autumn. Although the distance between Taunton and Bossington was only about 30 miles, 75 years ago it was quite an epic journey into quite a different world. Stage one would be the taxi ride to Taunton station from our house in Obridge, a hamlet on Taunton's outskirts. Thence a jolly porter, who for a tip of sixpence would stow the luggage onto the train waiting in the down bay. My father would then take me to see the engine, most probably a GW Prairie Tank. In this act, my father probably set in motion an interest in locomotives which is still very much alive to this day. And so stage two began, running out through Taunton West Yard, under Forty Steps, past Taunton School where I was to become a pupil a few years later, under Fairwater Skew Bridge and on to Norton Fitzwarren. Then right hand down a bit as we turned off the main line and on to the Minehead branch.

The journey is leisurely as branch line journeys should be, stopping at all the stations between Taunton

and Minehead and even doing a little shunting here and there. At Stogumber and Williton I distinctly remember the calls of 'ripe fruit, ripe fruit' by station staff as they endeavoured to sell punnets of strawberries or raspberries to passengers. Watchet usually had something of interest going on. Perhaps old *Rushlight* was unloading coal from South Wales or a slightly larger vessel discharging paper pulp or esparto grass for the paper mill. There was often a strong smell of burning around Watchet Harbour, as esparto grass caught alight very easily and fire hoses were kept run out ready for immediate action. Strangely, I can only recall seeing water in the harbour on one or two occasions.

Blue Anchor with its long line of beach chalets was passed and not long afterwards, looking out on the opposite side comes one of the finest views I know of anywhere – Dunster Castle sitting among trees on the low hills above the village. There might even be a game of polo in progress in the park. A few minutes later we chug into Minehead station with its immensely long platform.

Stage three is the transfer to the Minehead-Porlock bus, waiting outside the station. Oh yes, 70 years ago the GWR knew all about an integrated service. The changeover here was a simple operation as the luggage was collected and delivered later. By bus we went as far as Allerford, getting off not a hundred yards from the famous pack-horse bridge, one of the most photographed spots in the country. This is the last stage of the journey. The final mile to Bossington we walked – in my case probably partially carried by my father. But we wouldn't have left Allerford without calling at the Post Office as father knew the postmaster, and also looking into the blacksmith's forge beside the stream where without doubt a horse would be having its hooves re-shod.

About half an hour later we were at Olands front door. 'Ere you be then', beamed Will from behind his bushy moustache as we were hugged to Mrs. Floyd's ample bosom in turn.

Sir Richard Acland gave the Holnicote Estate, which included the villages of Allerford, Selworthy and Bossington, to the National Trust. Acknowledged to be one of Somerset's prettiest, Bossington with its thatched roofs, round chimneys and bulging bread ovens runs roughly alongside the river for perhaps

A delightful photograph, taken in 1915, of the cobbled pack-horse bridge at Allerford on the edge of Exmoor. (*Author's collection*)

half a mile, but its pride and joy was its magnificent giant walnut tree, reputed to have been six hundred years old. Unfortunately it had to be felled in the 1950s having become unsafe, but I remember it well.

In the 1920s village life continued exactly as it had for hundreds of years. We really had come to a different world. There was no electricity. Downstairs illumination was by paraffin oil lamps – not a lot of light but a very distinctive smell. In the bedrooms it was candles. Each bedroom had its washstand complete with basin, ewer, slop pail and chamber pot – but as compensation the beds had the most wonderful and unforgettable feather mattresses and pillows.

The toilet arrangements probably took the most getting used to as Olands was still using the medieval Mark 1 Type Earth Closet. This gloomy and cold draughty outbuilding was situated in a shrubbery on the far side of the lawn. If it should be occupied – not that anyone stayed longer than absolutely necessary – there was another one about a hundred yards down the garden. This was a timber structure with wide gaps

between the planks and multitudinous knot holes. Light and airy? Yes, up to a point, but definitely not a comfort station. A plus point was that it was light enough to read the toilet paper, usually the Daily Mirror or the Daily Sketch.

One other minor point was that you couldn't draw water from a tap on Mondays as there was only one small pipe supplying the village and it got overloaded trying to cope with washing day.

Across the way was the shed containing the Cider Press. It was always a disappointment to me that our autumn visits never coincided with cider-making time. It may have been coincidence or it may have been due to my parents' strict teetotal convictions. My mother frequently recounted the story of how her father, whilst assisting with the haymaking, was persuaded that newly brewed cider was quite innocuous. He rather liked it and refreshed himself copiously. The result was that he had to be brought home on the hay wain, thereby illustrating the awful dangers to those tempted by strong drink.

Many great rural characters lived in the village such as Will Floyd and his wife Doris. He was quite obviously a man of the soil with his weather-beaten features and bushy moustache, flat cap askew, collar–less shirt, corduroy breeches, leather gaiters and huge boots. Doris was a large motherly woman who invariably wore a long brown dress and the inevitable pinafore. They lived quietly and happily, Will tending his acre of well-kept vegetable garden, couple of pigs and some chickens. Produce would be sold in Porlock and each week a large wicker hamper of vegetables was sent off to Harrow School. Doris looked after their visitors, providing at least four large meals a day. How I remember those suppers of home-cured ham, home-made bread and pickled onions.

Amongst the villagers many stood out as unique country characters: Mr 'ook who suddenly built a bungalow in his orchard and established the Orchard Tea Garden, and Farmer Roll who had a parrot that called out rude things to passers-by. The locals insisted that his bird was a near relative of Long John Silver's Capt'n Flint.

Belief in fairies and pixies was quite widespread. Thus, it was generally agreed that Miss Quinton was a witch. I was convinced – broomstick or not. And she had a nasty-tempered black cat. Walkers on the hills frequently got themselves lost and the explanation was always the same: 'Ah, they was Pixie led'; nothing to do with the mists that would suddenly form out of a cloudless sky.

One could hardly call the front room of Miss Marley's cottage a shop, but it was as near as Bossington could get. Her main line was postcards, lemonade and sweets and she did a good line in Sherbet Dabs. Apart from all this she was licensed to sell stamps and tobacco.

Then there was the mysterious but well–educated man Harry Clare who lived in farmer Roll's hay loft. He helped out on the local farms but no one ever got to the bottom of his secret, just rumours: 'Came from London to get away from it all'; 'Crossed in love, so they say.'

But there was one particular character who I found awesome. Known as Carrier Floyd (Will's cousin) he combined a small transport business with being a sheep farmer. I mentioned earlier that we had left our luggage at Minehead station to be picked up and delivered later in the day. It was Carrier who did this with his old Thornycroft flat bed lorry. Probably ex-WD – it had solid rubber tyres. Now Carrier was a very large man, well over six feet tall, and he wore a full, bushy black beard. As he had a medical problem with his eyes he had to wear very dark glasses giving him a rather sinister appearance. Apart from this, when tending his sheep which roamed the nearby hills, he rode an immense black horse and wore a black cape which flowed out rearwards. All topped, of course, with a flat cap, the normal headgear for all occasions except Sundays when it would be replaced by a bowler.

In appearance Bossington still looks much as it always has done – except for the missing walnut tree. But things were starting to change slightly in the early 1930s. We were now coming by car. And a new type of oil lamp had been developed which combined an incandescent mantle with a wick and produced a powerful white light – and at about the same time a portable radio made its appearance. However, as far as Olands was concerned, the real leap forward came, I think, during 1935 when a new bathroom/toilet was built on over the kitchen – a great step forward but it was still several years before the electric came and the water supply improved.

Although the village looks as old world as ever, it is inevitable that people and their lifestyle have to change. No longer do they live out their lives in and around their native village, but move on – jetting around the world like everyone else! But on a summer evening as dusk falls, stroll down to where the wooden bridge crosses the river, stand in the middle and close your eyes, listening to the babbling brook. A dog barks in the distance over Porlock way. An owl hoots, probably from Farmer Roll's barn. Country smells waft around, wood smoke and damp soil, manure and garlic. There's a hint of tobacco smoke and quiet voices. It's my father and dear old Will sitting on the old bench seat in the garden at Olands having a quiet pipe and chat at the end of the day. 'It's been hot today, Will, and I fancy Bossington is a very relaxing sort of place'. Will considers this, then 'It's something I can't say I've ever suffered from'. A longish pause and a few puffs before 'I hear that old Josh Stenner over Lynch way has passed on'. 'Ah, and so he has. Never mind, it couldn't be helped and he was only digging his potato bed the day before. Old Josh was ninety eight'. 'Well, I suppose we better be getting in. These gnats is beginning to bite'. 'Well, goodnight Will, see you in the morning'. 'Goodnight Fred'.

(*right*) Everybody seems to be enjoying themselves on the local stagecoach, which is being driven by James Hewart. This was a major attraction for rides in and around West Somerset. (*R. Kingsley Tayler/ Peter Lockwood collection*)

(*left*) The stage-coach is seen here being put onto a lowfit wagon for an onward journey to its new owners, c.1961. On the right is Alfie Littlefield, on the left is Stan Dean, and at the back are Percy Howe and Ernie Crockford. (*R. Kingsley Tayler/ Alfie Littlefield collection*)

(*right*) HRH the Duke of Edinburgh visited Minehead on his West of England tour in October 1952. He is seen here being welcomed by dignitaries at the station. A special train was provided which was hauled on the branch by a class 4300 No.5376.
(*R. Kingsley Tayler/ Peter Lockwood collection*)

(*below*) A crowd of onlookers patiently awaits the Duke's arrival in the rain.
(*R. Kingsley Tayler/ Peter Lockwood collection*)

Steve Martin

With my parents' family history it was always likely that transport of some type would have a big influence on my life. Grandfather on my father's side was coxswain of the lifeboat at Minehead and during the summer months worked for P&A Campbell's White Funnel Fleet so perhaps this explains my greatest regret, that the *Bristol Queen* was allowed to go for scrap in the late 1960s.

However, it appears that grandfather Stevens who worked on the permanent way at Washford has left a greater mark. My mother, Ena Stevens, worked for the GWR on Minehead platform up to 1951 and with the birth of my sister Elizabeth, this meant from a young age we were regular visitors to the station and were well known to station staff. I can vaguely remember being offered a footplate trip on what I think was a 5100 Tank but declined.

Following my mother's death in 1959 we still used to visit the station but this time with my next-door neighbour Charlie Pinkham who kept racing pigeons. Every Friday afternoon we would bring them to the station to be transported by train to their race destination. This used to take place in the cycle shed where the booking office is now.

Growing up in Minehead, the railway was a focal point of the town. I can remember the change from steam to diesel and the withdrawal of goods services. I also recall seeing No. 46229 *Duchess of Hamilton* on the turntable prior to transporting it to Butlin's. I

used the trains fairly infrequently myself although my sister travelled daily for a couple of years to Taunton College and she remembers that the train would always be held for her by the station staff. I last travelled the line during December 1970 in the last week of passenger service and thought what a shame that this would be the last time. Happily this has not been the case and whilst we should enjoy the West Somerset Railway for what it now is, we should, when possible, try to recreate the Minehead branch as it was.

I often try to recollect memories and mention Dunster; it was there the stationmaster used to keep chickens next to the railings. Also I recall my aunties would try to convince us when leaving Taunton that we were on the Barnstaple train. It was only when we got on to the Minehead branch we would be convinced.

The locomotive type which really takes me back to my childhood is the Hymek diesel. Summer Saturdays in the 1960s involved the Lido swimming pool, either swimming or sunbathing and always, it seemed, to the sound of a D7000 in the station. To hear D7017 at Minehead now brings a vision of those days. Hymeks were also involved in getting days off school in 1964 when The Beatles were filming *A Hard Day's Night* on the railway. The school authority gave everyone time off to go to the station and even now some of the outbuildings near the station have John or Paul painted on the walls. One wonders what this wall is now worth?

Hymek D7047 with second man Melvyn Baker leaning out of the window, on the Minehead to Cardiff train in August 1964. (*Melvyn Baker collection*)

On a nice sunny day in Minehead, a diesel multiple unit is about to leave the station. The indicator board shows it is going to Weston-super-Mare. (*Trevor Martin collection*)

(*left*) Driver Roy Cross is seen here on a Hymek at Minehead. Roy was well-respected as an engineman and a legend at Taunton shed. (*Melvyn Baker collection*)

(*below*) D7029 at Minehead in 1970 waiting to leave with a Saturdays only through train to Paddington. North Hill on the right looks misty. (*John Cornelius*)

A Hard Day's Night

When the Beatles made *A Hard Day's Night* in the spring of 1964 it was their first film. Alan Porton who worked for British Rail for 23 years, was working in the movement office of the division manager's office at Paddington station, dealing with excursions and special trains. He recalls a request to plan a special train from London to Minehead – he believed it was for three or four days for filming purposes. It was not until later that he was informed it was for the Beatles and that secrecy was paramount.

The Beatles were obviously hot news and the worry was that fans would flock to Paddington station during the commuter period and bring the station to a halt. So in military fashion it was agreed that while the train would start and terminate at Paddington, each day it would stop en-route to pick up and set down the 'Fab Four'. As far as Alan can remember, Hanwell, Ealing Broadway and West Ealing were the chosen stations where the VIPs would arrive by car and be collected at the end of each day.

The arrangements went well with few problems and so far as he can remember the specials ran to time – obviously word did get out about what was happening and fans learnt quickly of the stations concerned but insufficient to cause any major problems. All the filming took place on the Minehead branch and Alan was obviously eager to see the film as he was in some way involved with the film.

The sequence of the Beatles running alongside the train was made at Crowcombe station. Seeing the crowds controlled by the police reminds one of how popular the Beatles were at that time and still are. Certainly Minehead had never seen anything like it before or probably ever will again. We have included a selection of photos that bring back those days again, when Beatlemania was part of Minehead's history.

One of the trains the Beatles travelled on is seen here at Dunster. The Hymek diesel looks like D7076. If so it survived the cutter's torch and resides on the East Lancs Railway. (*Margaret Gould, née Hunt, collection*)

(*left*) Mayhem on the track at Minehead as The Beatles hit town. Who were the two young girls being escorted off the track?
(*R. Kingsley Tayler/ Peter Lockwood collection*)

(*right*) The two policemen seem to be enjoying themselves as do the crowd of youngsters, who have come to welcome John, Paul, George and Ringo.
(*R. Kingsley Tayler/ Peter Lockwood collection*)

(*above*) A very young Alison Atkins has a day to remember with John, Ringo and Paul, and is that Wilfrid Brambell in the background?
(*R. Kingsley Tayler/ Mike Chilcott collection*)

(*left*) Wilfrid Brambell with that smile that brings back great memories of the classic TV comedy series, *Steptoe and Son*.
(*R. Kingsley Tayler/ Peter Lockwood collection*)

(*above*) Looking out of the carriage at Minehead station, 'The Fab Four', with Wilfrid Brambell (who played Paul's grandfather in the film), look as though they are having a great time. (*R. Kingsley Tayler/Mike Chilcott collection*)

(*right*) No, it's not gricers running to get a train number. The *Hard Day's Night* celebrities have just hit Minehead. (*R. Kingsley Tayler/ Peter Lockwood collection*)

Margaret Gould, *née* Hunt

I first came to Dunster station when my father Jim Hunt (his real name was Frederick) was promoted from porter at Churston in Devon to signalman at Dunster in 1941 or 1942. I was a young girl at the time and found the moving an exciting time. I have lived in Dunster ever since.

My father was happy in this job and never looked for promotion. My mother Eleanor, was the crossing keeper at Sea Lane, Dunster where the family lived during and after the war. It was very isolated then, just a few cottages nearby. I used to help mother at the crossing and remember Roy Hobbs working on the station. On a Sunday there were two trains in the morning and four to six in the afternoon.

One day father slid on the woodwork, put his arm out to break his fall and damaged it. He rang down for me and I worked the box under his supervision. It was the early days of the NHS and we had to phone up the doctor to come and have a look at father. We had to get a relief man out to work the box. Father travelled to Exeter where his shoulder was put back and he was off work for a while until it healed.

I also took the tickets for father when he was working on his own and at that time he would have to manually operate the gates, by the box, especially in the early morning or evening. Sue Cole, the stationmaster's daughter, sometimes helped me; she used the ticket punch. She would come to our cottage to have a bath as they had no running water.

In the evenings passengers would sometimes be met by cars; one local man even worked on the Stock Exchange in London. One lady drove up to meet her husband and I told father 'She's wearing her nightie'. Dad replied 'She's in evening dress'.

I remember taking father his tea once whilst he was on duty. He was across the line in the goods shed, loading wood. I was normally not allowed in there. It was the first time I had been in there and being a nosey chatterbox I asked lots of questions, one of which was 'What's behind the door on the side of the goods shed?' Dad replied, 'That's where the ghost lives'. 'What ghost is that?' I said. 'It watches us at work here in the

shed', came a reply from one of the men who were tidying up. Thinking that I was being teased and only half believing that there were such things as ghosts, I then asked what this ghost looked like. Dad replied that when working quietly in the goods shed some workmen had seen a man dressed in a reefer style jacket and a peaked cap watching them. He looked like someone from the early 1900s. The other men in the shed agreed with what my dad had said. I asked them if anyone had spoken to the ghost to find out who he was and why he was there. I was told that if you spoke to him or approached him he would disappear. When the ghost made its first appearance I don't know but a lady porter employed at the station refused to have her meals in a room off the goods shed because of the ghost. Alone on the station at night, father would sometimes hear a sound of a door closing, but nobody was seen. Could it have been the goods shed ghost taking a stroll?

Years passed and we had left the railway and the Dunster goods shed had gone to the back of my mind, until one day some time after the re-opening of the Minehead line. Someone asked me if the goods shed at Dunster was haunted. This person told me that two chaps were working in the goods shed and saw a man watching them. They spoke to him and he faded away which scared them. The description of the ghost was the same that had been seen all those years ago.

Dunster was one of the busiest stations on the line during the last war with soldiers based at Dunster Beach Camp. There were six soldiers to a hut and one stove. Mother would be told of troop trains leaving Dunster in the middle of the night and she would inform the soldiers who controlled traffic and opened the gates. When leaving the area the troops would march down to Dunster station, often in the dark. A lot of troop trains ran after the service trains had finished. They wouldn't run as far as Minehead because the locomotives could run round the train via the goods shed. There was very little illumination on the station, it was only lit by oil lamps, as was our keeper's cottage. Before the Americans came in 1944 I remember the following regiments: The Engineers, Fusiliers, Green Howards, Somersets, Devonshires and the Parachute Regiment.

Though the army were at Dunster beach we could go onto the beach to play or swim. We were warned not to swim when the tide was going out because of a strong current. Barbed-wire covered the coastline, with pillboxes at intervals along the top of the beach. The whole of the beach to the low tide mark was planted with posts, to prevent German aircraft from landing. On the top of the beach were some concrete platforms on which stood rocket guns. One day when these guns were being fired, my mother found a dog hiding in our home; this dog was terrified of the guns. After the dog was befriended by my mother, it always came to hide in our place when the guns were firing.

At the beach end of Sea Lane was an old shack occupied by an old man called Tim and his dog. In his early days he had been a jockey and helped to train horses. Tim had another talent, he was an excellent painter, and could draw a horse faster than one could sign a name. When he needed money he would take his paintings to Minehead to sell.

Everything came in by train, petrol rationing saw to that, and of course everything went out by train – timber from the saw yards, pit props from Exmoor's woodlands, which were sent to the coal mines in trucks that had brought in coal. Provisions for the shops and newspapers came on the passenger trains. Tomatoes and other produce were sent to market from local nurseries, and cattle and sheep were transported in and out from the local farms on foot. Horses and sometimes bulls travelled in horseboxes attached to passenger trains, with the horseboxes loaded in the cattle dock. I sometimes helped push the horsebox into the sidings. An extra siding and loading bay was constructed to cope with the traffic created by the war.

I can remember a police car coming to Sea Lane Crossing to tell my parents that an ammunition train was due the following day and that the station and sidings had to be cleared for this train. It must have been early in the year for there was a frost and a covering of snow. The police car had slipped back on the crossing and father had helped push the car back on the road. I was very excited to see this goods train slowly work its way along the line with soldiers on the locomotive, trucks and the guard's van, all with fixed bayonets. Mother didn't think it so exciting. She commented 'I hope they don't drop any of it when unloading or we shan't be no more'.

Father was in the Home Guard and on a manoeuvre one night took the station from a rival platoon. Another time on night movements near Blue Anchor the ganger fell in a ditch full of water and he said: 'All these years I've done this line and I never knew this bloody ditch was here'.

Besides the ganger and his deputy, there were six on the local line gang who, every morning, would check the wooden keys. They would lift and pack the permanent way, and every day reach parts of their length using their own trolley. You could hear the clonk, clonk of the hammers from quite a long way off. This was often done just after the local goods train had passed. They were responsible for the Minehead to Washford section.

(*left*) Old Tim is seen here outside the hut he lived in at Dunster beach, c.1946. He looks a character and what marvellous stories he could tell about his life in and around the marshes of Dunster.
(*Sue Illingworth-Kay collection*)

Of course I tried to get candy from the American soldiers: 'Have you got any gum chum?' One American did try it on with my mother who at the time was carrying a three aspect lantern. 'You come near me and you'll know what this one's like' said mum, indicating the lantern. It wasn't all fun in those days, some of the Americans were sent to Shepton Mallet prison and I believe at least two were executed there.

My mother retired from the crossing on medical grounds and I took over as crossing keeper for about five years. I was 18 years old. I had to be on duty while trains were running and sometimes this was for 24 hours, though this was very rare. The last train in summer normally passed at 22.15 and the first in the morning at 07.00, but sometimes it turned up at 06.30.

Once my mother was in her night clothes awaiting the early morning train. It had left Blue Anchor but where was it? She could see it up the line; the footplate crew had stopped to pick mushrooms in the fields.

We knew when a train was on line, for in the cottage we had a signal machine which repeated the bell codes between Dunster and Blue Anchor signalboxes, but we were not allowed to touch this machine. Our crossing cottage had been specially built for this job and although the surrounding area sometimes got flooded, our cottage never did. One time the rains actually flooded the ballast out and it spread into the nearby fields. Dad would ring up Dunster Castle at times of heavy rain and threatened flooding. They could control the flow of the local river and divert it onto the marshes near Blue Anchor and save the railway from flooding.

When I was crossing keeper the gates were normally closed against the road as there was little traffic and often the road users would operate the gates. There was always one who wouldn't leave the gates as they found them. One night, in the war, the Americans used a vehicle that was too wide for the gates and took everything with it including a field gate with dimensions of 12 feet across.

After mother died and I was still crossing keeper, father would phone up and ask if I wanted to go shopping as there was then a shop on Dunster Marsh. He said the train was running late and this would give me time to go shopping. Also drivers would hold the train until the gates had been operated, and I would get a lift into Minehead and come back on the next train. I even used the goods train to do my shopping.

I kept a fire burning in the cottage for most of the year for that was how I had to cook. Stationmaster at the time was Sid Cole and Ron May was the other signalman who later moved on to Exeter after promotion. We even had a relief signalman come up from Paignton. In later years, signalmen straight out of college, with no portering experience, worked opposite father. It was difficult to keep a second signalman as the young men wanted to move on.

I left the railway in the early 1950s on medical grounds, though my rheumatism did clear up. When living on the Marsh where my husband was the local postman, I had a dog who often disappeared, but he'd follow the river down to Station Road and visit father in the signalbox. I only had to phone father to find out where he was. My father, Jim Hunt, retired at 66 years of age. I have fond memories of those days and it is nice to recall the branch line as it was. It was a way of life for our family.

(*left*) In 1950 Dunster station was flooded. Here we have Sea Lane Crossing keeper Margaret Gould up to her ankles in water. (*Margaret Gould, née Hunt, collection*)

(*above*) A locomotive is seen in the background, as a station photograph is being taken at Dunster, c.1940s. From left to right, sitting down: Eleanor Hunt (crossing keeper), Sid Cole (stationmaster) and Louie Mogg (porteress); standing up: Tommy Kemp (signalman), Roy Hobbs (clerk who became a famous entertainer under the name of Roy Van Dyke), Jim Hunt (signalman) and Percy Hobbs (porter/shunter). (*Margaret Gould, née Hunt, collection*)

(*right*) In the signalbox at Dunster are signalmen Jim Hunt, on the left, and Norman Snell. What a lovely view it must have been with the trees and meadows in the background. The lamps on the shelf are worth a fortune in today's market. (*Margaret Gould, née Hunt, collection*)

Class 2251 No.2213 is about to depart from Dunster with a passenger train for Taunton. Note how clean and tidy the platform is. (*R.K. Blencowe collection*)

A fine view of Dunster station looking towards Blue Anchor with the signalbox on the right and the goods shed on the left. (*Margaret Gould, née Hunt, collection*)

John Cockrem

The railway was a big part of my young life at Dunster Marsh. It became a good playground for all the kids in the area. I am afraid my memory of events is a lot better than names involved. My first early memory came from a trip in my pushchair down to Dunster Beach. My mother would have to struggle with those heavy gates to get the pushchair through and I remember the bumpy ride over the lines. On one of those beach expeditions, a local boy, Bill Mandley, got into difficulties while swimming and later the local paper accused my mother of running along the beach making peculiar noises. She was trying to attract the attention of the boys on shore but in her panic couldn't get the words out. However, her noises did some good because Albert Taylor, a local scout, was able to drag Bill to shore and give resuscitation; Bill survived.

The railway was like a magnet to most of the boys in the Marsh area, although in the depressed 1930s very few had any chance of riding on the train. There are the memories of rushing down to the station to watch the polo ponies being unloaded and watching the coal trucks being shunted into position to be unloaded by local colliers. Sometimes Harry Loyd would give us a ride in his truck if we helped him bag up the coal. We would see loads of sheepskins and animal skeletons being loaded for glue, we were told. We would get quite a few rides on returning lumber wagons and also collect some of the abundance of horse manure for the garden which was good stuff.

One serious accident did occur at the Sea Lane Crossing. A local farmer's son, Tony Williams, was leading his horse and cart through the crossing gates (a difficult task) and was hit by the train. I think in the confusion of gate operating, the horse moved off without instruction and Tony was seriously injured, but survives to this day. Unfortunately the horse died. My mother said: 'You will not go near that railway again'.

Later, a lot of activity occurred in Sea Lane when the powers that be decided to build chalets on Dunster Beach. We boys would go to the site and pick up wooden offcuts for the fire. At this time there was an increase of traffic over the crossing. If you happened to be there when a vehicle wanted to cross and you opened the gates for it, you might get a reward of a penny. Eventually this became common knowledge to all the local kids and through the school holidays, weekends and bank holidays there would be an unwritten arrangement of first come, first served. If you had a friend, you could each operate one gate and share the proceeds, but, if you were alone, it was hard work. It meant opening one gate, letting the vehicle through and shutting that gate behind you. Then running across the track to open the other gate, let the vehicle through, and shutting the gate again. It was important to make sure that the gate was closed to stop a second vehicle creeping through at the same time which of course was not very profitable. We boys were learning the tricks of the trade and in one season I managed to acquire 15/- which was a great help to my new bike fund. This situation carried on for some years and the traffic would increase year by year. However the railway authorities, realising the dangers, put their own gatekeeper on the job and alterations were made, with new signs erected – 'STOP LOOK LISTEN'. This was the beginning of the end for us boys as gatekeepers. The authorities even had the cheek to build a bungalow on site to accommodate a full-time gatekeeper. Bill Greenslade one of my gate partners, would later go on to be a fireman on the line and Stan Potter, who lodged with him, would become a driver. Quite a lot of rail personnel would be accommodated in the Marsh area, their names forgotten, except Mr. Lake who finally retired and settled nearby.

One day, my father and I were at the station when a train came in. My father knew the driver and stood at the cab door talking to him. The driver said to me: 'I bet you would like a ride on the engine'. I was already taking steps to climb in when he said: 'Oh no, not now, some other time, later'. I remember the feeling of great disappointment. It was over 50 years later when I got the chance to ride on the footplate. Ian Grady obtained permission for me to ride with him on a run to Bishops Lydeard and back. It was a fantastic experience and I remembered the promise of that driver many decades before.

It was always a source of great excitement when the Flying Circus came to Dunster. It would be held in a twenty-acre field just near the Sea Lane Crossing. Needless to say, Sea Lane was cast into chaos. The traffic would often get jammed in the crossing area. We boys would leave the gates alone at this time – no point in manning the gates if they were held open. Instead we enjoyed the spectacle of the stunt flying, wing walking and parachute jumping from old biplanes like Sopwiths, Bristols and Avros.

I also remember an amusing incident on a trip to Taunton with my parents. As the train left Watchet my father said: 'Look out for the Queen Bee launch ramp as we pass Doniford Military Camp'. The Queen Bee was a radio-controlled experimental plane used for target practice. The launch ramp was built over the track towards the sea and the train would pass under the structure. 'There it is', said father, and in a second we had passed under it. There then occurred a terrible thunderous crack; everyone in our compartment ducked forward, almost bumping heads with the people in the opposite seat. The carriage did a little shudder, with exclamations of 'Oh, god, what the hell is that'. I looked at my dad for reassurance; he was sat there with a big grin on his face. A quick look out of the window and I caught a glimpse of the culprits. Right along the seaward side of the track were these huge anti-aircraft guns. They had fired a salvo at some target in the channel. Remarks, after recovery, were like: 'It shouldn't be allowed'; 'we should have been warned'; 'what a waste of money'. My dad was still

(*above*) Young fireman Melvyn Baker in the cab of 0-6-0PT class 5700 No.9647 at Dunster in 1962. (*Melvyn Baker collection*)

laughing at the reactions of some people and turned to look out the window to hide his mirth. Our ears were still ringing when we arrived at Taunton. These are just a few incidents I recall in connection with the Minehead branch.

The majestic sight of the 27-lever GWR standard pattern Dunster signalbox, which opened in 1934 and closed in 1971. How many cups of tea were drunk in there? (*John Pearce collection*)

(*above*) After chatting with the Dunster signalman, the driver of class 5100 No.4159 checks everybody is on board for the final dash to Minehead. (*Margaret Gould, née Hunt, collection*)

(*left*) Snow is on the ground as an unidentified steam locomotive and train are seen at Dunster, c.1955. You can just sense the cold and wonder if the snow has not affected the working of the signal wires that run near the centre of the picture. (*Margaret Gould, née Hunt, collection*)

Stan White

I lived at Taunton and started work on the railway in 1939, firstly as a greaser, subsequently becoming a cleaner, goods fireman, then a passenger fireman and finally a driver. The Minehead line was very busy involving goods as well as passenger services, especially on summer Saturdays when it was necessary to bring into operation two intermediate signalboxes to maintain the services, as well as local trains. There were also through services from the North as well as from London Paddington. I recall one occasion working a passenger train on a Saturday, approaching Watchet where the line encountered a series of bends. To my horror, as we were proceeding along, I saw an elderly couple walking along the track. I immediately blew the whistle as hard as I could and the gentleman pushed his wife onto the bank. They both looked horrified as we passed by.

On another occasion, early one morning, we were passing the caravans which were situated along the side of the line at Blue Anchor when I saw a lady emptying the necessary; she gave us a wily smile.

An incident which I recall was when running into Dunster station one day with a through service. The train staff had to be given up but nobody was there to receive it, so I slid the staff along the platform where a tea chest was standing, only to see it go straight through the tea chest.

When working on the branch line with a Mogul class 63xx engine to Minehead, it was quite an effort to turn the engine for its return journey working. You would have to place the engine far enough forward on the turntable so that you could pull a ramp down behind, then back the tender on to it, to enable you to turn the engine.

The stations on the line were always kept in first-class condition and there was keen rivalry among the different staff to win the annual contest for the best-kept station award. Also, you often saw railway staff selling fresh fruit to passengers as the train stood in the platform.

I enjoyed my life working on the branch and the 46 years I worked on the railway.

Fireman Stan White (left), who spent 46 years on the railway including the Minehead branch, is seen here with his driver Harry Bishop. (*Stan White collection*)

Fireman John Crocker poses for the photographer as his locomotive, a class 4300 No.6398, enters Blue Anchor station with a permanent way train. (*John Pearce collection*)

A view of the small yard at Blue Anchor, looking towards Minehead, c.1950s. North Hill is misty and Conygar Tower appears on the left-hand side. The siding is still connected and there are far more holiday chalets than there are now. The railwayman appears to be giving a lick of paint to a post. Note the smart condition of the gates and fences. (*Joe Moss/R. Carpenter collection*)

An early photograph of Blue Anchor station of which only the main building and platform now remain. The signalbox has certainly changed. The second platform was added in 1904. Look at the period dress of staff and passengers. (*John Pearce collection*)

GREAT WESTERN RAILWAY.
— NOTICE —
ALL PERSONS ARE WARNED NOT TO TRESPASS UPON THE RAILWAYS OR STATIONS OF THE COMPANY AND NOTICE IS HEREBY GIVEN THAT PURSUANT TO THE PROVISIONS OF THE COMPANY'S ACTS EVERY PERSON WHO TRESPASSES UPON ANY SUCH RAILWAY OR STATION IN SUCH MANNER AS TO EXPOSE HIMSELF TO DANGER OR RISK OF DANGER RENDERS HIMSELF LIABLE TO A PENALTY OF FORTY SHILLINGS AND IN DEFAULT OF PAYMENT TO ONE MONTHS IMPRISONMENT FOR EVERY SUCH OFFENCE
BY ORDER

Judy Hall

In the late '50s and early '60s, for part of my school holidays, I would stay with my family at Blue Anchor. A highlight of these times would be a trip on the train with my Nan, Kate Rawlings, to either Taunton or Minehead for lunch. Nan and I would be dressed in our Sunday best for this outing and Nan's best was usually a two-piece suit or costume with matching handbag and shoes. On this particular day we went to Dorrien's in Minehead, which as I remember was an elegant place with faultless service and the whitest of tablecloths. Lunch over, we walked back to the railway station for our short journey home. I was first onto the train and as Nan followed, disaster struck. In true Cinderella style her burgundy leather shoe slipped from her foot and bounced under the carriage. In spite of several helping hands, it refused to be retrieved. 'Not to worry, Mrs. Rawlings', said the stationmaster, 'we'll get it when the train has gone and send it up on the next train'. To solve the problem of having only one shoe, Nan took off the remaining shoe, together with her stockings and put them in her handbag. With suspenders tucked up neatly in her corset, Nan and I carried on with our journey to Blue Anchor station. We walked along the seafront, Nan happily barefoot, to Aunty and Uncle's house. When the next train was due Uncle Ron was despatched to collect the shoe, which arrived with a luggage label bearing the correct name and address tied securely to the heel. The guard handed it to my uncle and I can only imagine the conversation between them, but knowing my uncle it was colourful. I work at the Buffer Stop Shop on Minehead station and often smile to myself when a customer has dropped something onto the track, remembering my Nan's burgundy leather shoe over 40 years ago.

This is a Bristol LS bus of the Western National fleet, crossing at Blue Anchor. The bus route ran via Old Cleeve. Next to it is a baby Austin and another baby carrier to the left of that. The steam engine is a class 4300 No.6398 on the up line facing in the down direction and is probably hauling an engineer's train. (*Walter Harris collection*)

It is summer at Blue Anchor as two young brothers stand on the platform with their buckets and spades in the 1950s. Looking closely at the lad on the right, is that a train engine on his jumper? (*Walter Harris collection*)

(*right*) Token exchange with the signalman at Blue Anchor in the 1950s during the passing of an up train. The photograph was taken by Mike Haynes, now one of the regular volunteers in the station office at Minehead. (*Mike Haynes*)

(*below*) Class 4575 No.5563 leaves Blue Anchor in the up direction on a very wet and misty day. The telegraph poles are still in situ but not in use. (*Walter Harris collection*)

(*left*) No.4157 of Taunton shed heads a down train out of Blue Anchor during BR days. One cannot miss the lamp on top of the level crossing gate. (*West Somerset Steam Railway Trust collection*)

(*below*) The crew take a breather before taking 0-6-0 No.2261 away from Blue Anchor with a passenger train on a stopper to Taunton. (*R.K. Blencowe collection*)

A general view of Washford station looking towards Watchet. The tall lamp standards seemed to have served their purpose. What a pity the goods shed has not survived. In this shot a couple of mineral wagons can be seen on a well covered piece of track. (*Walter Harris collection*)

Roy Pitman

My first experience of the Taunton to Minehead branch was in the summer of 1942. As a member of the Wincanton Platoon of the Somerset Army Cadet Force, I learnt that the annual camp that year was to be held at Dunster. We were conveyed by army lorry to Taunton station where we were ushered aboard a train in the bay platform. It consisted of non-corridor stock with a 2-6-2 GWR Prairie at the head. The weather was brilliant, absolutely sweltering, and conditions on the train were very uncomfortable. I well remember the only way we could get some relief from the heat was to pull down the window blind, hold it outside the window at an angle and deflect air into the compartment. On arrival at Dunster station we were marched down to Dunster beach where we were billeted in what were pre-war (and post-war) holiday chalets.

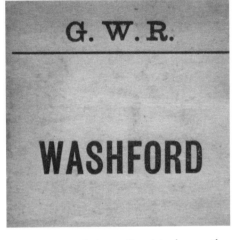

My next trip on the branch was many years later in the late 1960s. At the time I was the manager of an insurance company in Bridgwater, and Minehead was in my area. With time being no object on this particular occasion, I decided rather than drive to Minehead I would go by train. I parked the car at Taunton and boarded a DMU for the journey. No problem at all, just a leisurely amble down to the terminus at Minehead. Business concluded, I caught another DMU for the return journey to Taunton. Everything went fine until the train was between Crowcombe and Bishops Lydeard where it came to a halt. After quite a long wait, passengers were eventually informed by the guard that a tree had come down on the line and would be removed as soon as possible. Some two hours later I arrived back at Taunton station, hungry, thirsty and not in the happiest of moods.

Little did I know that some 20 years later, I would be very much concerned with that very railway. As a member of the Somerset & Dorset Railway Trust I was appointed stationmaster at Washford, the Trust's headquarters in the early 1990s, and a position I held until 2003. During those most enjoyable years I got to know the railway very well. There were still Prairie Tanks and DMUs running which brought to mind memories of past experiences. I am now involved with the West Somerset Railway, which is a wonderfully friendly and efficient organisation. Long may it continue.

(*right*) Washford station, taken from the A39. A cattle market once stood next to the station; there was also a signalbox here, which closed in 1952. Mike Palmer was a member of the Somerset & Dorset Railway Trust which is based here and its museum is well worth a visit. Mike was a tireless worker for the Trust for many years, and it is thanks to him and many others that the SDRT has gone from strength to strength. He is sadly missed. (*Mike Palmer*)

Barbara Burdge

My dad Stan Bedford joined the Western Region as a driver in 1952, having been made redundant at Highbridge on the Somerset & Dorset Railway. At first he found himself referred to as 'that S&D or Midland bloke', but things soon calmed down and he settled into his routine, learning all the new routes.

We had travelled to Devon and Cornwall for our holidays down the main line, but the branch lines were a mystery to us. Dad fell in love with the Minehead branch. He loved the scenery of the line with the Quantock Hills and its beautiful sea views. He took mum, my sister June and myself on a trip in the spring, when all the wild flowers were in bloom. There was plenty of wildlife on view and we even caught a glimpse of some deer. He couldn't wait to see our faces when we saw places like Crowcombe, Stogumber, and Blue Anchor with their lovely flower gardens. I think dad's favourite spot on the line was Watchet, with its little harbour, where he could sit and watch the tide come in while Mum pottered around the shops.

One year my sister took her two little girls Martina and Maria to Blue Anchor for a caravan holiday. Dad happened to be working the line that week and arranged to sound a special whistle as he went into Blue Anchor station. When he returned from Minehead they would be waiting on the platform and he would give them some sweets and ice cream money. Also he would hand over anything mum had sent them, to save my sister June from having to cook; talk about meals on wheels!

There is a story about dad's mate, driver George Brooks, who was gathering some blackberries on the side of the line somewhere on the Minehead branch. He had stepped on what he thought was a solid piece of ground. As he got off the footplate, which was next to an overgrown patch of brambles, he found himself

Driver Stan Bedford, on the left, seen with his fireman on a Midland engine 3F No.43792. Stan spent a number of his 48 years as a railwayman on the Minehead branch. In later years he used to visit Washford for S&D reunions. (*Barbara Burdge collection*)

in a concealed water tank. The water broke his fall but the air was blue while his fireman pulled him out.

Alas for poor dad he earned the only black mark on his railway record when working on the Minehead branch. As most people know, the tablet giving the right of way on a single track section of the running line is taken from the machine at the start of the journey and returned to the machine at the end of the section. Dad's fireman volunteered to collect the tablet while dad was checking out something on the steam locomotive. The right away was given. 'Tablet on board?' asked dad. 'Yes', said the fireman and away they went, but on reaching the end of the section the tablet was not in the pouch. Apparently it hadn't been secured properly and had fallen off the footplate. The fireman was very upset and wanted to take the blame, but dad said 'This is a lesson for you to learn; the driver of a steam locomotive is always in charge and I should have checked the tablet was present before we left, so the fault is mine'. This resulted in his only reprimand in 48 years service to the railway. He must have had something on his mind that day as he was such a stickler for the rules.

We were all sad when the line closed, but delighted that it has been saved. A few years later we were able to continue to have many happy journeys plus the added joy of attending the Somerset & Dorset reunions over the years at Washford. When dad heard that the S&D engine No.88 was at Minehead, he was delighted. On a visit to Minehead my mother had a friend whose grandson, Richard Jones worked on the West Somerset Railway. We called in to see him while we were there and after a brief chat we went round to the seafront after inspecting No.88, promising to call in again on the way home. When we arrived back we found that Richard had arranged for dad to travel on the steam engine that was hauling our train back down the branch. Dad was delighted and we left him on the engine chatting happily to the crew. Mum was quite happy to travel in comfort, but I was green with envy.

A passenger waits as a three-coach DMU set draws into Washford with a Taunton to Minehead train in 1963. (*E.T. Gill/ R.K. Blencowe collection*)

Jack Reeder

My father loved his working life on the railway. My family and I, George Reeder, are very pleased that his railway memories were recorded by the *WSR Journal* before he passed away. Here are his lovely memories of those days.

Ex-Watchet shunter John (Jack) Reeder talks to Graham Stagg about the working of Watchet Harbour from the 1940s.

I first met Jack, the former Watchet shunter, on Watchet station during the 125th anniversary celebrations. In the course of our conversation he kindly invited me to call at his home and hear about Watchet station and harbour during British Railways days. Jack was born in North Yorkshire in 1911, the son of an ironstone quarryman. Life was far from easy in the North East, which was in recession throughout the 1920s and 30s. Jack met and married a Durham girl and during the 1930s worked in a limestone quarry and spent three years in the regular army. He was recalled to the colours on the outbreak of war and joined the Second Royal Horse Artillery, serving in the Middle East and Italy until being posted to Doniford Camp near Watchet in 1945. When he was demobbed on 5th November 1945 Jack was anxious to restart life with his wife and four children whom he had barely seen for six years. Bill Knight, the then Watchet shunter, was about to retire, so Jack applied for and was appointed to the position at just over £4 for a 48-hour week. The family could not move to Watchet at once so Jack lodged in the town but after two years or so he obtained housing about half a mile from the station. Until goods traffic was withdrawn from the branch, Watchet was the most important station on the line, serving as it did a town of over 2,000, a busy port and the large paper mill. The staff consisted of ten, a stationmaster (Jack served under six until closure in 1971), goods clerk, junior goods clerk, booking clerk, junior booking clerk, female porter, a Goviers Lane crossing keeper, a shunter and two further male porters. Even at such an important

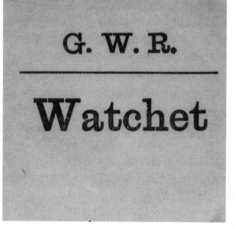

G. W. R.
_____
Watchet

station the stationmaster did not have his own office, simply being allocated a desk in the station building and having a lockable cabinet for the station books. The life of the goods yard revolved around the paper mill and the harbour. Such was the volume of traffic to the mill that a Watchet special would run at 07.00 from Taunton, bringing what was called mileage traffic. This consisted of empty vans, waste paper and dyes and could be up to 18 wagons at a time. From 6 to 14 van loads of paper would then be sent away from the mill. The train arrived at Watchet at about 08.30 and Jack recalls that provided he let the crew fry their breakfast on a shovel on the locomotive they were a co-operative lot from Taunton, often main-line men transferred to a less demanding task. The harbour was a busy place and all traffic was rail-hauled. Pulp for paper mills all over the West came from Sweden. Then there was esparto grass, also for the paper mills, from North Africa, and coal from Penarth in South Wales, by the paper mill's own boat, the *Rushlight*, which made two or three trips a week. Finally coal was brought in by Smith's Barges of Bristol. In addition to supplying the needs of the Kentsford Mill for raw materials and coal, the needs of inland mills such as Silverton in Devon were supplied. General traffic included vehicles, guns and supplies for Doniford Camp, sugar beet traffic from Parsonage Farm near Watchet, paper and supplies for the Exmoor Paper Bag Company in Anchor Street and bulk supplies of writing paper and envelopes for H. W. Clark. Coal was delivered by rail for the town's domestic use and up to 6 truckloads a week came from Yorkshire for the town's gasworks. In addition to its own traffic, Watchet had the line's only wagon weighbridge which was installed mainly to weigh wagon loads of pit props on their way from Dunster yard to coal mines up and down the country. Lastly, Watchet was often called upon to stable wagons when other yards were over run with traffic, like Washford during the monthly cattle market. In truth, the Watchet layout was inadequate for the traffic on offer, a factor which helped in its downfall. The dock's two steam cranes, which had their own rail track, could load up to seventy trucks a day but customers would only take thirty at a time, which could lead to congestion in the yard. Shunting was mainly done by horses, both at the mill and in the yard. The horses, which were supplied by a local contractor, were also used for local cartage delivery. The yard layout was awkward, needing three wagon turntables and much movement of wagons by hand. Differing siding capacities made Jack's job of marshalling trains in the right order both a work of art and a nightmare. When an engine did arrive the crew had already been on duty for two hours and by the time they had a meal break and taken traffic to and from the mill, there was little time left for shunting before they returned to Taunton. At busy times a second crew would come out by passenger train. The dockers would work sixteen hours per day when the ships were in, so the rail staff had to follow suit, leading to much-needed but hard earned overtime. Watchet's signalbox closed in the 1920s, the goods yard being supplied with an intermediate token instrument between Washford and Williton. As passing trains at Washford was only practical if one was a goods train, in effect there was a single section from Williton to Blue Anchor on a line with fifteen goods and passenger trains in each direction. Shunting at Watchet forever delayed the working of the branch and the railway's telephones were often very warm between Jack's shunting cabin and neighbouring signalboxes. In the 1950s a former GWR director who lived locally suggested that Kentsford box be opened for one shift per day and the porters at Watchet were retrained to do the work but even so, shunting arrangements led to delays. These delays could reach epidemic proportions if a crowded troop train arrived at Watchet and the train engine had to run round. To get through the workload at busy times the rules were often bent and Jack recalls frequent fly shunting, which was very much forbidden. Sadly, this led to a man being crushed to death in Kentsford Mill when the points were wrongly set. Shortly after this, the mill received a Fordson tractor to assist in shunting. Derailments of wagons were frequent, due mainly to worn or defective point work. Such incidents would lead to the Taunton re-railing crew being sent out to Watchet. Another frequent problem was wagon buffers locking together during rough shunting, especially if the shunting engine misjudged the length of a train and hit the stop blocks. Once a boat arrived in the harbour

the dockers would get straight to work on unloading. The cranes could load 5 wagons an hour and as Jack's shunting engine from Taunton did not arrive until 08.30 the dockers, who started at 06.00, might have anything up to 15 trucks ready for marshalling by the time shunting could start. Each wagon could take 13 tons and working at full rate the dockers could unload a 1,800 ton boat of pulp in four days. Because of its greater bulk esparto grass took up to six days. The wagons were all opens and as the pulp and esparto grass had to be kept dry it all needed to be sheeted and roped down which was very hard work indeed. A tarpaulin could weigh 1 cwt. and had to be carried up onto the wagon, spread out and roped down. Staff were sent from as far away as Taunton to assist but even so, casual labour was frequently employed. It is hard to think such arduous and low paid work can ever have been but a last resort, especially on cold, wet winter days, but the job had to be done. After sheeting down, all the wagons had to be weighed, which would block Goviers Lane Crossing for long periods, a practice

Shunter Jack Reeder, complete with shunting pole, May Norman and porter Stan Amies at the crossing at Watchet. (*George Reeder collection*)

which led to endless complaints from the Town Council. Finally the train could be marshalled. Engines could lift a maximum of 18 wagons of pulp but up to 30 of the lighter esparto grass. The limit of 30 wagons was set by Crowcombe loop (Watchet's loop could take only 20 wagons or 19 with a tender engine) and the 18-wagon limit was set by Crowcombe Bank. Even with these limits, engines often arrived at Crowcombe very short of water after the long climb from Williton. Jack recalls that on one occasion two wagons of esparto grass caught fire on Crowcombe Bank and further damage was only averted by some swift shunting at Crowcombe station. Jack's problems did not end with the organisation of the yard gang and getting the wagons marshalled in the right order; he had to decide when to let a shunting engine go to Williton for water (in conjunction with the signalman, of course) and what wagons to put on which train. At

Shunter Jack Reeder, on the left, with two other station staff at Watchet, c.1949. In the cab of a class 2251 No.2266 are fireman Harry Kirkland (left) and driver Gordon Richie. Note the ex-ROD tender. (*George Reeder collection*)

busy times the two branch pick-up goods would call at Watchet to collect wagons as well as the Watchet special and possibly another special in connection with the boats. Remembering that Watchet loop was only 20 wagons long, a lengthy pick-up goods might have to stand on the running line while wagons were attached, delaying the whole branch and making Jack decidedly unpopular. Then every wagon had to be marked to show what was in it and where it had to go, and defective wagons green carded for repairs, although often there were so many defective trucks that repairs were delayed. Jack also had to ensure all the trucks were swept out before use, another job for which casual labour was used. Finally, at the end of a day's shunting there was the paperwork. Three books had to be marked showing what trucks had passed through Watchet, inwards and outwards books and a separate book for mill traffic. To add to this, Jack had to order any special trucks, which included low loaders for military traffic, and estimate the number of trucks needed for the next day's traffic. Many was the time in the wagon shortages of the 40s and 50s that Jack was so short of wagons that he had to frantically telephone to other stations on the branch to grab any surplus wagons they might have. One of Jack's more pleasant tasks was to distribute a £10 Christmas box given by the paper mill to the branch line staff. Unfortunately, so many people knew about this gift and expected their share that it got rather diluted in its distribution. I asked about the large tin shed in Watchet yard that used to cover one track just by the 6-ton crane. It turns out that this was originally used to load and unload supplies of paper and esparto for Kentsford Mill. After the mill had its own sidings installed the shed was used mainly by Exmoor Paper Bag Company and by local coal merchants to bag their coal in the dry. The rundown of the goods traffic started when the mill began to distribute its wares by its own lorry fleet. That put paid to the Watchet special and left the branch with just two pick-up goods. Shortly after this, the mill switched from coal to oil electric generation, the oil coming by road. Other mills did the same and the coal boats stopped calling at Watchet. The gas works switched to North Sea gas so the coal traffic from Yorkshire ceased. Then the pulp traffic switched to road. To the users the logic was inescapable, rail wagons could take only 13 tons of pulp and needed shunting and marshalling during their journey, often getting lost and taking an age to reach the mills. An articulated truck with 3 trailers each taking 20-25 tons of pulp went straight from harbour to customer, often making two or three journeys a day. One tractor had 3 trailers, one loading, one unloading and one in transit, allowing the harbour to increase its output of pulp to deal with 7,000 and 8,000-ton boats. The rail layout would have been overwhelmed by such size. Finally, the railway decided that the movement of a light bulky substance like esparto was not economic and shed the traffic, concentrating the remaining traffic at Taunton. Jack became redundant for the first time when Watchet yard closed, and became a grade two porter at Watchet station, which included booking office and parcels duties. Even in the 1960s Watchet could take £500 in a day with a heavy parcels traffic and servicemen from Doniford travelling by train. Chickens, pigeons and other small livestock were still handled by passenger train in sizable quantities. By 1968 BR was ready to introduce conductor guards on the branch and Watchet was to become un-staffed so Jack was again redundant. This

time he went to Minehead as a senior porter, starting on 25 March 1968. What is now the Buffer Stop shop was used as a left luggage office and a luggage in advance store. By 06.00 on a summer Saturday coaches would be arriving with people for Butlin's, but they could not enter the camp until 13.00 so they left mountains of luggage at the station. While the coach drivers slept in readiness for the return journey, the departing people from Butlin's would leave their luggage at the station to get in a last minute walk along the promenade or a bit of shopping. The 1d in the slot loos did a roaring trade! It is rather depressing to think that with tens of thousands of customers travelling to Butlin's each year, BR just could not be bothered to run a special train, or build a simple station at the camp, which is next to the railway line, or even encourage campers to travel by branch train, which few ever did. Faced with such apathy the inevitable happened in January 1971 and Jack became redundant for the last time after over 25 years of railway service.

The last coal trucks into Watchet for the West Somerset Coal and Trading Company on 1 July 1964. In the photo, from left to right, are Cecil Stone (builder), railwayman Jack Reeder, Percy Williams, owner of the coal company, and Reg Cornish, an employee of Mr. Williams. (*R. Werren collection*)

(*above*) Unloading esparto grass shipped to Watchet from North Africa and destined for Silverton Paper Mill, Devon by rail, c.1950s. Driving the tractor is Tom Tudball whilst Stan Amies is walking beside the railway trucks ready to apply the handbrake. (*B.A. Butt/Ben Norman collection*)

(*left*) It is the late 1950s at Watchet Docks. Ron Cornish, on the left, and Leon Kidson are earning some overtime by covering a truck full of esparto grass with one of the heavy tarpaulins, before it becomes part of a goods train to work up the branch and onto the main line. (*Leon Kidson collection*)

(*above*) Outside Watchet station are signalman Sam Jacques, Gertrude Amies (collecting for flag day), shunter Jack Reeder and stationmaster Henry Payne. (*Donald Amies collection*)

(*left*) Watchet permanent way ganger, Jack Clavey, who worked on the branch, is certainly enjoying a glass of beer at *The Bell*. He was a jovial character who was fond of a game of skittles and a few pints with his mates. (*Ben Norman collection*)

With Watchet in the background, Pannier Tank No.5760 heads a Taunton to Minehead train on 20 July 1955. Hope no ladies have their washing on the line with the amount of smoke coming from the Pannier! (*Stanley Creer/Transport Treasury collection*)

A very early view of Watchet showing the Chapel on the right of the photo. It is post-1882, as the running lines are now of standard gauge and the signalling is still *in situ*, as are the tall signalbox and goods shed. (*F.G.S.G. collection*)

The many cars suggest that something special was taking place at the Methodist Chapel in Station Road, Watchet, c.1930s. On the left at the back of the photo is the station waiting room. There are GWR trucks full of coal in the goods shed and on the left are the hoist chains for the hand crane. A number of children can be seen; two of the girls in the middle of the road appear to be playing a game. (*Ben Norman collection*)

The Wharf at Watchet with the Esplanade across the harbour and an interesting selection of pre-grouping owner's wagons in Watchet yard. These include the Midland Railway, North Eastern Railway, Hull and Barnsley Railway and of course the Great Western Railway. (*F.G.S.G. collection*)

A wonderful shot of two horses shunting a Southern Railway wagon with Arthur Sully in charge, at the turntable at Splash Corner, Watchet. Note the harbour in the background and the lady leaning up against the railing. (*F.G.S.G. collection*)

Chris Sheppard

My late great grandfather William Knight started work at Watchet station sometime around 1890. He worked for over 50 years at Watchet station as a messenger boy, and later as a porter and a shunter. He was quite a character during his time. His nickname was 'Whistler' Knight due to the fact that he was always whistling the tunes that he played on his euphonium with the Watchet Town Band. He had ten children, seven girls and three boys. One of them was my grandmother, the late Hilda Bale, who often spoke about her father. Because he had such a large family to support and did not earn much money working on the railway, he had several allotments situated along the side of the railway line at Watchet. My grandmother said that she and her sisters would be given the task of taking a packed lunch of sandwiches and cider to William, which often took time, as they never knew which allotment he was on. He was also able to buy coal at a reduced rate, which was a perk of working for the GWR. William Knight retired from working at Watchet station just as the Second World War started. He came out of retirement after a year or so to work back at the station as the younger staff were being called up for war service. William retired again in 1945 and died in 1952.

If it had not been for Dr. Beeching my parents would probably never have bought a car, as we went every-where by train. It wasn't until after British Railways closed the line in 1971 that my father learnt to drive and bought a green Singer car, registration number WYD 892H. In about 1960 my father would take me on the train to Minehead, where we would walk to the Lido open-air, sea-water swimming pool. I would spend some time in the shallow end of the pool and I used to love to watch my father diving off the boards at various heights. But to me, the best thing was to watch the steam locos in Minehead station run around their trains and prepare to make the journey back to Taunton. There were large and small Prairie and Pannier Tanks and even the odd Mogul tender engine. They could be seen from the back top row of seats next to the wall of the pool, which backed onto the railway land.

During my time at Watchet Primary School I enjoyed many school outings, but the one which stands out most in my memory was probably the shortest in distance from the school. It was a bright March morning in 1964. Several classes of pupils, including mine, were lined up in the playground. The teachers tried to get us in some sort of order before we walked down the hill and along South Road to Watchet railway station. We were going to see a special train go through Watchet station; this train was conveying the Beatles to Minehead. We were all lined up and well back from the platform edge. We waited expectantly for the train to go through the station hoping to see our 1960's pop idols. The train arrived, but did not stop; instead the cream and chocolate carriages hauled by a clean green diesel hydraulic loco of the D63xx class flashed through the station with shouts of 'I saw John' and 'I saw Paul' but in truth the train was so quick we could not see anyone. It is a memory of my childhood that I still cherish.

Two photographs of shunter William (Whistler) Knight's elegant daughter Hilda Bale. On the left, she is seen with her daughter Josephine on Watchet station in 1931. Look at the old gas lamp behind them. On the right, she poses for the camera in Station Road, Watchet, with a nice array of wagons on the right-hand side, c.1940s. (*both photographs Josephine Sheppard collection*)

At the time I thought that the loco was of the D800 series Warship class, but my Uncle Clarry, who was a railwayman at Taunton, told me it was a diesel of the D63xx class. The Beatles were on the Minehead branch to do some filming for their first film, *A Hard Day's Night*, and at least one scene in this film was shot on Crowcombe station. The scene is the one where the Beatles are running along the platform, shouting to an old gent sitting in the train: 'Could we have our ball back'. Paul and John were shouting, while Ringo was riding a bike.

Growing up in the 1960s, Watchet was a wonderful place to live. I used to walk up the old Mineral Line. I would also go fishing in the river, or catch fish off the West Pier with a rod borrowed from a friend. My favourite thing of all was to catch an early train from Watchet to Taunton to go trainspotting. I suppose I would have been about 12 years old when I was first allowed to go to Taunton on my own. I would sometimes meet my cousin there and we would spend all day watching trains in our school holidays and on some Saturdays. I would underline the locomotives I saw in my copy of *The Observer's Book of Railway Locomotives*.

One such day was 21 April 1969. After riding in one of the branch line's blue and grey liveried DMUs, I arrived at Taunton where I saw a feast of diesel hydraulics including Hymek D7017 which we often saw on the Minehead branch in the 1960s. There was a Warship class D815 *Druid*, one of my favourite diesels, and some Westerns, which included D1014 *Western Leviathan* and D1034 *Western Dragoon*.

Often when I went to pay the conductor/guard for my 6/- return ticket, payment would be refused. 'Buy an ice-cream for yourself' was one answer I got from a conductor. Receiving only 10/- earned pocket money per week and with a model railway to run, it was a real bonus not having to pay. Little did I realise at the time it was probably a ploy to show the ticket numbers were down and one more reason to close the railway.

It must have been around 1967 that I recall one train journey back from Minehead to Watchet. I had gone to Minehead on my own earlier on a summer Saturday morning. The ride back to Watchet stands out in my mind as the train was made up of about 10 maroon liveried Mark 1 coaches hauled by a smart blue Hymek diesel hydraulic loco with full yellow ends. I stood at an open window, leaning out and watching the loco all the way back to Watchet. The most enjoyable part was right at the end of the journey with the loco's wheels screeching as she made her way around the curves on the approach to Watchet. If my memory serves me correctly I think the loco was D7061 with a head code of 1A38 which made it a Paddington-bound train, possibly the 11.15 from Minehead.

After doing my school homework I would often cycle down to Watchet station to watch the DMUs arrive and depart. One evening around 1968 I met my cousin Alan in Watchet and we decided to cycle over to Williton station to watch the trains cross over on their way up and down the branch. We arrived just before the trains and sat on a bench seat. The duty signalman Harry Horn came out of Williton signalbox and invited Alan and me into the box. He showed us all the levers and instruments in the box and how they worked. It was a warm summer evening and the light was fading fast. With the glow of the lights in the box and the kettle warm on the stove, it made for a very atmospheric view of life at the station.

Most days I would either walk or cycle with four or five school friends over the hill from Watchet to Williton Secondary Modern School. Some days in the warmer months, instead of going to school we would take the footpath by the side of the school and go to Williton railway station where the group of us would get on the train to go to Taunton. After paying for our half-priced tickets and armed with our sandwiches and drinks flasks we would walk up to the cricket ground to watch Somerset play. On one trip around the mid to late 60s, Somerset were playing the touring Pakistan XI. After getting off the train at Taunton we stopped at a shop on the way to buy a bottle of Corona fizzy drink in a glass bottle for two shillings. You got 6d back when the bottle was returned. This would be part of a pre-planned money-making scheme. At the cricket ground we would collect as many empty Corona bottles as we could and carry them back to the shop and collect four shillings on the empties. On arrival at the cricket ground we watched the Pakistani players practising in the nets. We retrieved their cricket balls when they flew over the nets and for our troubles the Pakistani players gave us cardboard bat-shaped souvenirs with their autographs printed on them. After clubbing together to buy a scorecard we would settle down to watch the cricket match until about 16.00 when we would make our way back to Taunton railway station to catch the train back to Williton. The usual remark from my mum on these occasions would be: 'you're late'; the usual reply would be that I went to my friend's house to see his model railway.

I still enjoy my days out on the WSR and it is nice to have memories of an era that was special in my life.

(*left*) Watchet station staff outside the station goods shed in 1935. From left to right: Joe Hunt (porter), Arthur Sully (horse-drawn goods delivery driver), and William Knight (shunter), who gave over 50 years' service to the railway. Unfortunately, we do not know the names of the two lads on the wall. (*Chris Sheppard collection*)

(*below*) The rear view of the Lifeboat House (now the public library) in Station Road Watchet, c.1933. Look at the board above the right-hand side of the fence with the name of Gladis Lewis GWR carting agent. On the far right you can see some railway trucks on East Wharf and who is the young girl? (*Jack Binding collection*)

(*right*) A late afternoon DMU, snowbound in February 1963, just before the bridge leading to Watchet recreation ground. Several passengers including Jack Binding alighted here and walked across the allotments into Watchet. Eventually the train got through to Minehead. (*Jack Binding collection*)

(*below*) Three coaches are lined up outside Watchet station opposite the Chapel, c.1950s. The first two could be Leyland chassis with Duple bodies and the third possibly a Dennis Lancet with a Lee body. Could the coaches be for a Sunday school outing? The Vauxhall on the left looks interesting. (*Donald Amies collection*)

Two GWR 2-4-0s, Nos 212 and 213, at Watchet in July 1912, when there was a public demonstration of the Angus automatic train control system on the Mineral Line between Watchet and Washford. These two locos were used on the test runs. Robert Binding is one of the gentlemen on the footplate, and on the ground wearing a flat cap is Tommy Peel of the Ritz Cinema. (*F.G.S.G. collection*)

2-6-2T class No.6113 coasts into Watchet station with a passenger train for Taunton. (*John Pearce collection*)

(*left*) Driver Ken Cridland is enjoying a yarn with guard Walter Thyer at Watchet station on a last day special on 2 January 1971. (*John Cornelius*)

(*left*) It appears railwayman Stan Amies is supervising the passing of an 0-6-0 on a goods train at Watchet, c.1950s. He is also keeping an eye on a couple just behind him. You can tell this by the shadows cast in front of him. (*Donald Amies collection*)

(*above*) What a great photo of some of the Watchet Home Guard on parade, at their weekend camp on the Brendon Hills. From left to right: Joe Hunt (porter), Joe Lee (postman), Jack Goostrey (lorry driver) and Stan Amies (porter). (*Ben Norman collection*)

(*right*) A very old coach at Doniford, being used as a Baptist Mission Room. This coach was situated on the left just inside the metal gate which now leads to the sewage plant on Doniford Farm. The person looking out of the coach appears to be wearing their Sunday best hat. (*F.G.S.G. collection*)

Trevor Martin

Trevor is a West Somerset man born and bred. His late grandfather Harry Symonds worked on the Minehead branch starting as a porter on Williton station. Before this he worked as a porter at Bratton Fleming on the Lynton and Barnstaple narrow gauge line. Living at Bideford, Trevor reckons his grandfather travelled to work via standard gauge from Bideford and narrow gauge from Barnstaple. One of his references for his position at Williton came from the Bideford, Appledore & Westward Ho! Railway. He later became a signalman at Williton. Trevor's mother Phyllis can remember being allowed to pull the levers in the box with her father's help. In 1926 when she was nine years old, her father obtained promotion to station-master, though he stayed on at Williton until the end of the general strike. Sadly Harry died before he could take up this position.

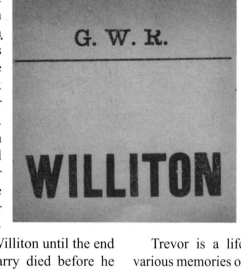

Trevor's uncle Charlie ran a fruit and vegetable business in Williton after the war. Charlie lived in Highbridge House next to the station and unlike the station, Charlie's home had running water. He allowed the railway staff to obtain water for the all-important cup of tea. In return the GWR granted Charlie a licence to sell fruit on Williton station to passengers on the passing trains. His staff would walk along the platform carrying the fruit in large baskets, shouting out what they were selling. This licence ceased with the end of the GWR in 1948. On 2 January 1971, the very last day on the Minehead branch, a member of the family, Edward Martin, repeated history by selling fruit to passengers on the station.

Trevor is a life-long railway enthusiast and has various memories of the branch. He recalls travelling up to London via Taunton in 1953 to see the Coronation decorations. He used to do the short trip to Blue Anchor to spend a day visiting his auntie's caravan, or when he worked at Blue Anchor Bay Garage. On one trip on a diesel unit, the guard, who was at the front of the train collecting fares, gave Trevor the nod allowing him to press the buzzer in the guard's van. He also gave the driver the right away for a train from Stogumber to Taunton – a lot of excitement for a young lad. In the 1960s Trevor spent time with Harry Horn the signalman at Williton when he was on duty. Harry talked about Bob Hensley the stationmaster who was a stickler for keeping the station spotless. On one occasion Harry had polished the waiting room door handle and the stationmaster came to inspect his work and was not impressed; he had to do it all over again. When keeping Harry company, Trevor was allowed to operate the levers in between trains, always using a duster. When trains were due he could shut the gates or when dusk approached he could light the gas lamps on both platforms by pulling the chains on each lamp.

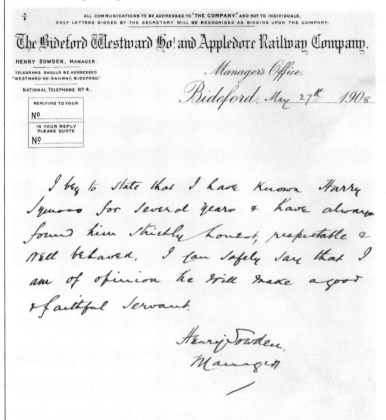

Trevor also used the line to visit relations in Taunton and to get around West Somerset. He was very sad to see the Minehead branch close as it was a way of life for everybody who worked or travelled on the line. He later worked as a volunteer at Watchet station on the West Somerset Railway.

(*right*) Trevor Martin's grandfather, Harry Symonds, looking very smart. Unfortunately, he died in service at a young age whilst serving as acting signalman at Williton box and did not live to take up his promotion to stationmaster. (*Trevor Martin collection*)

(*left*) Signalman Harry Symonds in Williton signalbox in the 1920s. The signalman's duster is seen hanging on a lever. (*Trevor Martin collection*)

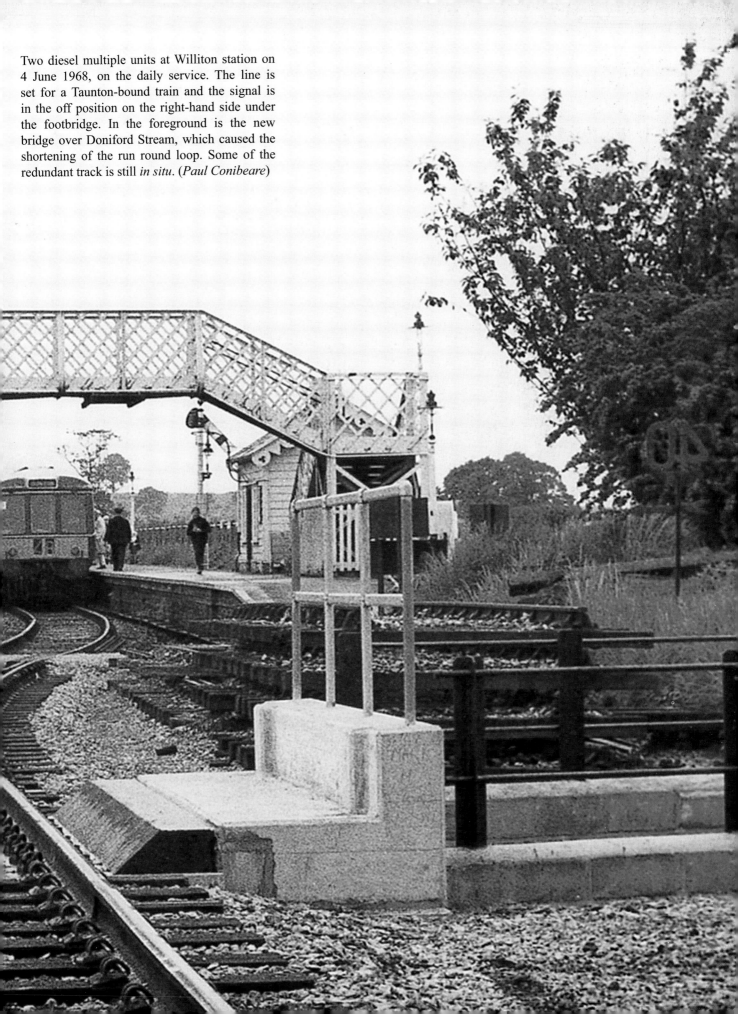

Two diesel multiple units at Williton station on 4 June 1968, on the daily service. The line is set for a Taunton-bound train and the signal is in the off position on the right-hand side under the footbridge. In the foreground is the new bridge over Doniford Stream, which caused the shortening of the run round loop. Some of the redundant track is still *in situ*. (*Paul Conibeare*)

(*left*) A class 4575 loco approaches Williton with a down passenger train, c.1950s. You can understand the reason for safety first as the gentleman stands in front of the signalbox. Note the water tank and the signal protecting the up loop line. (*Richard de Jong*)

(*below*) Aboard a First World War troop train at Williton station. Note the running boards on the carriages. We wonder how many of these brave young lads survived? (*F.G.S.G. collection*)

(*right*) An up train leaving Williton in 1966. An interesting shot as it shows the original length of the passing loop. Note the point rodding loop under the right-hand side of the road bridge. The footbridge must still be open as passengers are requested to use it to cross the line. (*Michael Hodge*)

(*below*) The permanent way looks immaculate as class 22 No.D6336 drifts into Williton station with a six-coach passenger train in 1964. (*Walter Harris collection*)

Ken Hill

Kenneth Hill is a local lad who grew up at Capton, near Sampford Brett. He attended school in Williton. In May 1960 Ken was interviewed by William Dilley, then stationmaster at Williton, for the post of lad porter at the station. After a further interview with the Taunton district inspector, Clarence Hawkes, he was appointed with a starting wage of £3. 15s. 6d. per week. When Ken started at Williton station it still had six staff, the stationmaster, two signalmen who were Harry Horn and Ralph Manning, relief signalman Ron May, porter Russell Hill, lorry driver George Smith and Ken. At that time Williton also controlled the next station up the line. The main buildings on the up and down platforms have stayed the same and though the footbridge has gone, a replacement at the time of writing was stored in the downside car park. A major change has been in the goods yard situated on the downside, which is occupied by the buildings of the Diesel and Electric Group, including the former goods shed and a shed formerly at Swindon Works, now used as a restoration centre. In Western Region days the passing loop was shortened in the 1960s when the river bridge was reduced to a single span. Now, as then, the level crossing gates are manually operated, though in Ken's time they were kept closed across the road and opened by road users as required. The signalman locked them from the box when needed for train operating.

Although railways are renowned for shift work Ken had regular hours. He worked between 08.00 and 17.00, had a five and a half day week, with a half day alternately on Wednesday or Saturday with porter Russell Hill. On summer Sundays the porter and stationmaster alternated and were paid overtime selling tickets. For operational purposes, evenings and all Sundays only, the signalmen were on duty adding the booking office to their signalling duties. Ken would meet the 07.25 from Minehead and the 07.30 from Taunton, which were due to pass at Williton at 08.03, although the first movement of the day was an empty coaching stock from Taunton to form the 07.25 from Minehead. Part of his work was cleaning the station, checking the toilets and brasses. This was followed by the next passenger train at 09.30 and then off to Jones Bakeries in Long Street to get whatever was needed for elevenses. Then, as now, railway personnel thrived and survived on a good old British cup of tea.

Every Monday Ken had the duty of dealing with the signal lamps, which could take up most of the day. It was not just a case of lighting the lamps and carrying them out to the signals; the replacements had to be cleaned, the wicks trimmed and the lamps filled up so they would burn for at least a week. There was the chance that a lamp could have gone out by the time the signal had been reached. Ken always carried with him a small piece of metal gas pipe

Signalmen Ralph Manning, on the left, and Harry Horn in Williton signalbox. With many years service between them, what stories they could tell about the branch. (*Iris Horn collection*)

with a knob on the end. A match would fit in one end so you could strike straight down onto the wick without burning your fingers. A head for heights was needed on the job, as you had to climb the ladder with a lamp in your hand, take out the original lamp, put the fresh one in and climb down.

On one summer's day Ken went to replace all the station lamps, which included the up distant at the Watchet end. His station colleague Russell Hill had assured Ken there was no need for protective clothing as it was going to be a lovely day. Ken walked up the line, got to the top of the down distant post, took out the old lamp and there followed a flash of lightning, one clap of thunder and down came the rain. Ken walked back through the rain; he was drenched and there was Russell who said 'I told you to take your bloody coat'. The stationmaster drove Ken home, waited while he changed and then drove him back to work.

The daily pick up goods train arrived at about 10.00 to shunt the yard on the down side, west of the station where the goods crane was now out of use. In Ken's time, along with Russell Hill and lorry driver George Smith, all the goods had to be manhandled on and off lorries. This included coal for Goodlands Coal Merchants, agricultural foodstuffs, fertilisers and machinery for Gliddons of Williton. Outward goods were more restricted and consisted of empty agricultural sacks returned to manufacturers and occasional specials, such as the time Gliddons sent a load of farm machinery to Ireland. Coal also came in for internal railway use for the station and signalbox fires; permanent way materials for the Williton-based gang and oil for the signal lamps normally sent in cans, and transported in the guard's van. Most important of all was being paid every Friday, when a strong box was sent to the stationmaster, which contained the wage packets.

Harry Horn, stalwart of the Minehead branch for many years, is seen here on the right with the DMU crew of driver Norman Penny and guard Harry Payne at Williton in the 1960s. (*Iris Horn collection*)

Goods in and out of the yard for local deliveries were taken by George Smith driving a petrol Bedford. Frank Short had the same vehicle at Watchet station. Later Williton had a 2½-ton Commer Carrier diesel and Watchet a 3-ton Austin diesel.

Ken recalls the local firm of Gerald Grandfield, that built poultry houses and sent the finished product out by rail. Two of these fowl houses would fit in an open wagon with their wheels removed so they wouldn't move about whilst in transit.

Ken well remembers one incident. The railway handled steel wire and mesh for a small fabrication firm called Tripods. These came in single sheets of rectangular shape and unwrapped. This time one slipped and went through Ken's right foot, two years after he'd put a garden fork through the same foot. Luckily the stationmaster was a trained First Aider and he cleaned up the foot so Ken completed his day's work.

Ken saw a good deal of local passengers and school children pass through Williton station, as well as seasonal traffic from St. Audries Holiday Camp. Locals took advantage of the 2/10d cheap day return to Taunton, which was available after 09.30 and before 16.00 Mondays to Fridays and all day Saturday. There were no taxis or public phone at Williton station so the phone at Bryant's Coaches in Station Road was used to phone for a taxi. In the summer months St. Audries Holiday Camp provided a courtesy bus as no regular bus service connected with the trains.

Local deliveries were made by George Smith with the station lorry which included having parcels of fish for the camp. Ken recalled that the station staff would ring the camp when the fish arrived and once when the station lorry broke down at the camp, the driver had to ring up for help. Later the camp manager, Frank Bissell sent an invoice to Williton for 4d to pay for the call.

St. Audries Girls School provided heavy traffic at the beginning and end of each term. Parcels were still sent by passenger train, sometimes quite heavy, and a parcel weighing machine was kept in the booking hall behind the main doors. Customers included Mr. Martin who had the farm next to the station, who sent out boxes of flowers. A dairy near Williton roundabout sent milk samples in metal containers to the Ministry of Agriculture at Yeovil. Other customers included St. Audries Garage, Gliddons General Stores, Parsons' and Hann's hardware shop and blind Jack who sent wicker baskets to his customers. Homing pigeons from all over the county were sent for release and once this had been done, the time and date were noted on a card which was returned to the owner, along with the basket.

Ken reminds us that the signalbox was still private and he was only allowed in on official business and even then he had to knock and await for permission to enter. Ken also remembers when the line was flooded at Williton. When the water came up to the platform level, the station staff carried on as normal, but no trains ran as the water level would have put the fires out in the steam engines. Of these engines Ken remembers the 2-6-2s which were based at Taunton. No.4157 which was based there in the late 1950s as well as Nos.6155 and 6157.

One day during the hard winter of 1962-63 Ken walked up the garden path to get his bike from the shed but the ice prevented this and he had to walk the three miles to work. Everywhere was iced up and he had icicles in his hair. Ken was greeted by 'You made it then!' Trains were running as the permanent way gang had salted the points to keep them operational.

At this time, Kentsford Loop was still in regular use and was manned by signalmen Sam Jacques and Jim Day. However, Leigh Bridge loop was only operated on a summer Saturday and often by one of the Crowcombe signalmen, Ron Cornish or Dennis Davey. The regular signalmen at Bishops Lydeard were Leon Kidson and Chris Palmer.

This leads us on to what Ken did after leaving Williton station. He became a booking boy at Taunton West main box in 1962 and also had a spell in the telegraph office on Taunton station. To get there, he cycled or used the Minehead branch train, operated by diesel units by then, or if necessary lodged in Taunton. One day, whilst based at the telegraph office, he returned from the locomotive shed having taken a message to John Forsyth. On his return he went to catch the last train to Minehead from the bay platform on the down side. He slipped on a greasy patch, put his hand out to save himself and dislocated his wrist. Though he didn't realise this until the next day, it delayed a planned move to Reading as a signalman; Ken was off work for three months. On return the district inspector, Clarence Hawkes, had Ken in Taunton West box, under supervision, pulling the levers to get his wrist operational again. Later he operated boxes in the Cheltenham and Gloucester areas before leaving railway employment to become a coach driver on continental services. Now he occasionally operates Minehead box as a volunteer and still drives buses for a living.

(*left*) This picture at Williton has been seen before, but we have now completed the names to the photo, so we feel it is right to be included. We are intrigued in what the occasion was for the photograph, c.1940s? From left to right: driver Charlie Warr, fireman Gilbert Millar, signalman Reg Cole, guard Sam Case shaking hands with stationmaster Bob Hensley, porters Alfie Palmer and Alfie Cross. (*Audrey Holcombe collection*)

(*below*) Seen here in 1969 are Williton signalbox and level crossing. The vehicles on the left-hand side are now classed as classic cars; they will be worth a few pennies today. On the right of the box is Highbridge House, former home of Trevor Martin's Uncle Charlie. (*Walter Harris collection*)

BRITISH RAILWAYS (WESTERN REGION) TRAIN SERVICE BETWEEN
TAUNTON — WATCHET — MINEHEAD
In operation June 11th to September 16th, 1956 (inclusive)

								Mondays to Fridays								FS	S	S
London (Paddington) .... dep	1150	...	5 30	9r30	...	11r30	...	1r30	...	3r30	5r30	7r30	1150	...				
Taunton .... dep	7 24	9 0	1025	1215	1 30	2 30	3 30	4 25	5 49	6 10	8 30	1015	6 55	7 24			
Norton Fitzwarren .... ,,	7 30	...	1029	1219	...	2 34	3 34	4 29	5 53	...	8 34	...	...	7 30			
Bishop's Lydeard .... ,,	7 39	910	1036	1225	1 40	2 41	3 42	4 35	6 1	6 20	8 41	1025	7 5	7 39			
Crowcombe................... ,,	7 47	918	1044	1233	1 43	2 49	3 52	4 43	6 10	6 28	8 48	1032	7 13	7 47			
Stogumber.................. ,,	7 53	923	1050	1238	1 53	2 55	3 58	4 48	6 15	6 33	8 54	...	7 18	7 53			
Williton.................... ,,	8 3	933	1059	1249	2 1	3 4	4 5	4 57	6 23	6 41	9 2	1045	7 26	8 3			
Watchet.................... ,,	8 9	939	11 5	1254	2 6	3 9	4 12	5 3	6 28	6 46	9 8	1050	7 31	8 9			
Washford .... ,,	8 16	946	1117	1 1	2 15	3 21	4 19	5 10	6 35	6 53	9 15	1056	7 38	8 16			
Blue Anchor .... ,,	8 21	951	1122	1 6	2 20	3 26	4 24	5 15	6 40	6 58	9 20	11 1	7 45	8 26			
Dunster .... ,,	8 27	956	1127	111	2 25	3 31	4 29	5 20	6 45	7 3	9 25	11 5	7 50	8 26			
Minehead .... arr	8 32	10 1	1132	116	2 30	3 36	4 35	5 25	6 50	7 8	9 30	1110	7 55	8 31			

					Saturdays only												
London (Paddington) .... dep	...	...	7r 0	7 30	9 35	9 35	11 30	1130	12 5	1r35	3r30	5r30	6 30				
Taunton .... dep	8 16	9 0	10 20	1140	12*40	1 5	2*20	2 55	3 25	4 45	6 15	8 30	1015				
Norton Fitzwarren .... ,,	8 21	...	10 25	...	...	1 10	...	2 59	...	4 49	6 19	8 34	...				
Bishop's Lydeard .... ,,	8 29	910	10 33	1151	...	1 20	...	3 6	...	4 57	6 26	8 41	1025				
Crowcombe................... ,,	8 37	919	10 42	12 0	...	1 29	...	3 15	3 48	5 6	6 34	8 48	1032				
Stogumber.................. ,,	8 43	925	10 52	12 6	...	1 35	...	3 21	...	5 12	6 40	8 54	...				
Williton.................... ,,	8 53	934	11 0	1214	...	1 44	2 55	3 32	4 5	5 21	6 48	9 2	1045				
Watchet.................... ,,	9 0	942	11 9	1219	...	1 51	...	3 39	4 11	5 26	6 55	9 8	1050				
Washford .... ,,	9 7	949	11 16	1226	...	2 2	...	3 46	4 19	5 34	7 2	9 15	1056				
Blue Anchor .... ,,	9 13	955	11 21	1233	...	2 7	...	3 53	4 32	5 40	7 7	9 20	11 1				
Dunster .... ,,	9 22	10 0	11 26	1240	...	2 14	...	4 0	4 38	5 47	7 14	9 25	11 5				
Minehead .... arr	9 27	10 5	11 31	1245	1 40	2 20	3 20	4 5	4 43	5 52	7 20	9 30	1110				

*—Through train between London and Minehead.
S—Saturdays only. FS—Fridays and Saturdays only
r—Refreshment Car between Paddington and Taunton

BRITISH RAILWAYS (WESTERN REGION) TRAIN SERVICE BETWEEN
MINEHEAD — WATCHET — TAUNTON
In operation June 11th to September 16th, 1955 (inclusive)

							Mondays to Fridays						F	S	S
Minehead .... dep	7 35	9 5	1050	1220	1 50	2 55	4 30	5 6	10 7	30	8 5	9 50	7 35	8 25
Dunster...................... ,,	7 40	9 9	1054	1224	1 54	2 59	4 34	5 10	6 14	7 34	8 9	9 55	7 40	8 29
Blue Anchor................. ,,	7 45	914	1059	1229	1 59	3 4	4 39	5 16	6 19	7 39	8 14	9 59	7 45	8 34
Washford .... ,,	7 50	920	11 5	1235	2 5	3 10	4 45	5 22	6 25	7 45	8 20	10 5	7 50	8 40
Watchet .... ,,	7 56	926	1112	1241	2 11	3 16	4 51	5 33	6 33	7 51	8 26	1011	7 56	8 46
Williton .... ,,	8 3	932	1119	1247	2 18	3 21	4 57	5 40	6 41	7 58	8 33	1018	8 3	8 52
Stogumber................... ,,	8 10	940	1126	1255	2 27	3 29	5 4	5 48	6 49	8 5	8 40	...	8 10	...
Crowcombe................... ,,	8 17	947	1132	1 1	2 32	3 35	5 10	5 55	6 56	8 12	8 48	1033	8 17	...
Bishop's Lydeard............. ,,	8 24	954	1140	1 8	2 40	3 43	5 18	6 3	7 4	8 20	8 57	1041	8 24	...
Norton Fitzwarren .... ,,	8 30	10 0	1146	...	2 46	...	5 24	6 9	7 10	8 26	9 3	...	8 30	...
Taunton .... arr	8 35	10 5	1151	1 23	2 54	3 56	5 35	6 15	7 15	8 31	9 8	1055	8 35	9 20
London (Paddington) ...... arr	12r15	1r25	2r50	5r35	6c15	7 15	...	9r 0	...	...	...	4 55	...	12r15

				Saturdays only									
				*	W		*						
Minehead .... dep	9 5	10 5	1040	1155	1220	1 35	2 15	3 0	4 20	5 5	5 50	6 35	7 50	950
Dunster...................... ,,	910	1011	...	12 0	1225	1 39	...	3 4	4 24	5 10	5 54	6 40	7 54	954
Blue Anchor................. ,,	916	1017	...	12 6	1232	1 45	...	3 12	4 30	5 16	6 0	6 46	7 59	959
Washford .... ,,	922	1024	...	1214	1238	1 51	...	3 18	4 37	5 22	6 6	6 52	8 5	10 5
Watchet .... ,,	929	1031	...	1225	1244	1 57	...	3 24	4 44	5 33	6 12	7 2	8 11	1011
Williton .... ,,	936	1038	...	1232	1250	2 4	...	3 31	4 50	5 40	6 19	7 9	8 17	1018
Stogumber................... ,,	943	1045	...	1239	1258	2 11	...	3 40	4 58	5 48	6 26	7 16	8 25	...
Crowcombe................... ,,	950	1054	...	1246	1 5	2 19	...	3 48	5 7	5 55	6 35	7 23	8 32	1033
Bishop's Lydeard............. ,,	959	1103	...	1254	1 13	2 27	...	3 57	5 17	6 3	6 43	7 31	8 40	1041
Norton Fitzwarren .... ,,	10 6	1110	...	...	...	2 33	...	4 4	5 24	6 9	6 49	7 37	8 46	...
Taunton .... arr	1011	1119	1140	1 10	1 26	2 42	3 20	4 15	5 30	6 15	6 55	7 42	8 55	1055
London (Paddington) .... arr		20	2r40	2r40	...	5r15	6 25	6 25	...	...	9r 5	...	...	...	5 0

S—Saturdays only. F—Fridays only. *—Through train between London and Minehead.
w—Through carriages Minehead to Birmingham (S.H.) and Wolverhampton (L.L.).
c—Change at Bristol (T.M.); limited accommodation from Bristol. Refreshment
Car available

Leon Kidson

I joined the railway in the mid-1950s and started work as a porter at Williton station. One of the signalmen there was Harry Horn. Our work included the transporting of livestock, which were loaded into trucks in the large goods yard at the Watchet end of the station. It was shunted by the local pick-up goods train that had come from Taunton and eventually returned there. I was lucky enough to work just the one shift, 08.00 to 17.00, a nice job for a railwayman and I didn't have far to travel as my family then lived in Williton.

After three years in this job I transferred to Stogumber in 1959, the next station up the line, still as a porter. Here, though, I was on shift work as I shared the duties with another porter. I cycled to work, for both shifts, in all weathers. The twisting road down from the A358 to Stogumber station was no problem. Later on I bought a moped. On the late shift I had to wait until the last train had gone to Taunton, then lock up the buildings, put all the oil lamps out, then I could go

home. Often on my journeys I would come across a great number of foxes, though I seldom saw the Quantock Foxhounds in action. Although there were no signals in the station area I still had to keep the lamps in the up and down distant signals alight. This involved walking out to both signals when they needed replenishing. Also Leigh Bridge Loop was still in use and I had to keep these lamps lit. The main goods we dealt with were agricultural stores and cattle which still went by train. A monthly job that I tackled was the accounts, though I received no extra pay for that. I worked a six day week and some Sundays.

At this time Stogumber still had a camping coach and both porters were in charge. Visitors came for a week, mainly by train, and they often sent their food requirements ahead which I ordered and arranged to be delivered. I also dealt with the money side for the hiring of the coach. When the visitors arrived I checked the list of contents of the coach with them and also before they left, to

The Stogumber village policeman, his bike leaning against the fence, with porter Leon Kidson on the right. A young lad has got Leon's porter's hat on and sits on a barrow with another gentleman, enjoying the sunny summer's day. (*Leon Kidson collection*)

Porter Leon Kidson, with a group of ladies who have enjoyed their holiday in the camping coach at Stogumber. (*Leon Kidson collection*)

not a very pleasant duty. There was no external phone but we did have a dedicated line that ran the length of the branch and a code to contact whoever we wanted down the line. The long demolished goods shed, which had a single line through it, dealt mainly with the local farmers who would pick up empty sacks, often ten at a time. They would take them home, fill them up with their own produce and have them weighed. They would then go out on the pick-up goods. The farmers kept their own records and they would bring up their produce in their own tractors and trailers. If agricultural produce had to be delivered I would arrange for the lorry from Williton station to be used. However, all the parcels had to be collected from Stogumber station.

My final move whilst working for the Western Region was to Bishops Lydeard, first as a porter and later as a signalman. Eventually I purchased a motorbike; it was still enjoyable to travel to work as there was still little road traffic about. This of course was a far busier station. For a start it had a stationmaster and a bigger goods yard than Stogumber. It was also double track from Norton Fitzwarren on the main line, and it was single from then on down the branch to Dunster. There were the pick-up goods to be dealt with which then moved on down the branch to Crowcombe. There was a private coalyard there but no free coal.

My duties once again included the signal lamps, the same walks in all weathers, and I had to do them on my own. I had no choice, train operation depended on the signals. About eight lamps would

prevent anything going walkabout. I held the key and arranged the water supplies which came from a well in signalman Harry Horn's garden. Most of the families enjoyed themselves and often left me a little tip for helping them.

At the back of the main building was a cesspit which is still there. This was always emptied by a road tanker and I had to decide when this was necessary,

Porter Arthur Rogers on Stogumber station with four young girls, who were staying in the camping coach for their holidays, c.1950s. We wonder who they are, as they must now be in their fifties. (*Iris Horn collection*)

need replacing when I walked in the Norton direction and I always carried a box of matches in case any of the lamps went out. When I reached the first lamp I always left the empty one behind, so the weight decreased on the way out and all I had to do on the way back was pick up the empties which weren't so heavy.

There was one porter at Bishops Lydeard covering one shift and I had my own porter's room on the down platform with my stationmaster resident in the dedicated house on the down side, though he seldom saw the trains away which was another one of my duties. The signalman's vacancy was an internal advert which received several applicants and I came out on top, I believe because of my previous experience and knowledge. I had to attend a written and verbal exam at Exeter St. Davids reached by rail via Taunton of course. I trained in Bishops Lydeard box along with an experienced man and when ready I was put through my paces by an examiner from Exeter. Thus I started my final job on the railway.

There were two signalmen employed in this box, my opposite number being Chris Palmer, and we worked an early or late shift, a six-day week with Sundays being extra. When trains weren't on the line I sometimes had to put the signal lamps out, a job I knew well. One incident I remember is when I despatched a train to Norton Fitzwarren. On my way back to the box I noticed a goods train coming from Norton which shouldn't have been on the line. The driver of this goods train must have passed a signal at danger but I was able to stop the train in time. The driver was well shaken up, but the incident was covered up.

I stayed with the railway until 1966 when I took up a job at Hinkley Point power station. However, I will always remember the extra work I did at Watchet Docks whilst working at Williton where Mr. Moore was the stationmaster. Esparto grass was received at the docks and loaded into the trucks. I would cycle after finishing my shift at Williton to Watchet to work overtime, paid at time and a half to get the wagons ready to move up the line. This included heavy work with the tarpaulins to cover the wagons. I often carried out this work with Ron Cornish and once finished, it was really nice to cycle home knowing I'd completed a good day's work.

Fred Hutchings

At the time of being interviewed Fred Hutchings was a sprightly 87 years of age, having been born in 1917 right opposite the church in Stogumber, where he grew up. He has very vivid memories of going to the then Richard Huish Grammar School in Taunton, starting when he was nine years old. Living in Stogumber, Fred travelled by train to Taunton and walked to and from the station in all weathers. Two weeks could go by and not a single car would pass him on the road. When he started in the junior part of the school the fees were £2.10s a term and for the senior part were £4 a term. Fred would leave home at 07.45 to catch a train at 08.00 or 08.10 depending on whether it was the winter or summer timetable in operation. He eventually got a bike so he could leave home a little later, leaving it in a shed at the back of the Railway Hotel which was at the bottom of the embankment on the down side. He would not leave it on the station as the GWR would have charged him for the privilege. His father was the local butcher, but he would not allow Fred to have a lift to the station, he always had to make his own way there. Children from Taunton School travelled on the train, as well as the girls for the other two schools in Taunton. They always travelled in school groups, but not always in the same part of the train. In those days Fred went to school six days a week, including 9.00-12.00 on a Saturday, the afternoon being used for sports. The pavilion they used looked as though it could fall down at any time and the washing facility consisted of a single cold tap situated outside.

Fred can just remember the Stogumber signalbox being pulled down. The stationmaster at the time was Bob Hensley who later took charge of Williton station and he was replaced by a Mr. Hutchins. The kids were known to each other on the train and up to 40 travelled into Taunton from all stations along the branch. Fred recalls the two regular guards were Fred Chidgey and Sam Case, they had to put up with a lot of cheek from the kids. Fred had a niece who attended a convent in Taunton and always travelled in the guard's van.

Three girls have their picture taken on the track next to the water tank wagon at Stogumber, which serviced the camping coach. Note the sign behind them, 2/8d. return to Taunton if you travel after 09.30. (*Iris Horn collection*)

I recall one of the railway guards had a son who kept the Promenade Hotel in Minehead. At one time they kept a parrot as a pet at the hotel and one day it escaped out to sea. The son was a strong swimmer and had to swim out to rescue the bird. On returning to the shore, his wife took the parrot from him and promptly pushed him into the sea for allowing it to escape.

Fred's father was not happy having to pay the season ticket for each term, which was normally between 13/- and 15/-. Although he tried to do as much homework as he could on the train he often got up to high jinks with the other schoolboys and they frequently had their names taken by the guard. They would put the girls up on to the luggage racks, especially the smaller ones. Or if they had a piece of chalk they could draw images on the windows. One day as they approached Stogumber, Fred managed to make it look like a crack in the window and called the guard. 'Sam, someone's broken a window' 'Oh dear, oh dear', came Sam's reply as he walked along the carriage with his notebook in his hand. Fred rubbed it off and made a quick exit as they pulled into Stogumber station.

In those days Stogumber had one long single platform on the down side of the line. On frosty or snowy mornings the locomotive would often struggle to get a grip on the rails as it started away from the station. The boys would take out one of the bulbs illuminating the train carriage and when they went under a road bridge they would throw the bulb at the brick arch and await the resulting bang. Then in the first week in November they would light a little demon as they got out of the

carriage and await the crack as it went off. It was all just devilment, nothing malicious. Those guards certainly had their work cut out and they must have enjoyed the school holidays.

On the return from Taunton in the summer timetable, one Minehead train left at 16.30 but did not stop at Stogumber, so Fred had to get off at Crowcombe and walk up the track to Stogumber. He got there at about the same time as the next train, the 17.10 arrived from Taunton. At Taunton the branch train would be held up if a London train ran late, including the Torbay Express. If Fred was the guard, he would seek out

No, not the end carriage of a train, but the occupants of the camping coach at Stogumber having their photo taken. (*Iris Horn collection*)

the wealthier travellers, unerring in his choice, who would be staying at hotels in Minehead, 'Carry your bags, ma'am?' and he would get a nice tip.

The goods siding, which formed a loop through the goods shed was never used as a crossing place. It was used mainly by farmers who would send off their corn. Incoming goods included concentrates for cattle feed, such as linseed cake. Horses and carts were used to deliver to the local farms especially by Tom White. Arthur C. Clarke was in Fred's form at school. He recalls the maths teacher saying to him one day 'Clarke, I've had a look at your book and it looks like a blasted spider has been in the inkwell and crawled all over it'. (Clarke is of course now a very famous science fiction writer).

All the local children went to school by train including brothers Les & Peter Robjohn from Porlock. They would board from Monday to Saturday, going home at weekends. The headmaster at Richard Huish took in six boarders. Fred can also remember the railway staff looking up the road to Stogumber village. If someone was late they would hold the train for you. Then there were the two Parson girls, who in the war, travelled to work by train every day. Percy Dudridge, a clerk, who came from the village, walked to the station, travelled to Norton Fitzwarren, changed there and caught a train to Wiveliscombe for his place of work.

A big influence on Fred's life was his father who started up a butcher's shop in Stogumber in 1909 and in 1926 purchased a shop in Holloway Street, Minehead from a man called Williams. When Fred left school in 1932 he went into the trade having always wanted to be a butcher. University was talked about, but his father said 'He had a university at home for him'. When he got married, Fred had a butcher's shop at Williton in 1939.

At one time there were six almshouses in Stogumber and Fred's father purchased all six to be used as storehouses, for in those days all cooking and heating was done by coal. His father would order a ten-ton truck full of coal, normally from the North Somerset coalfields. This would arrive at Stogumber on the goods side and a local haulage firm, Harold Jennings and Son, would spend all day transferring the coal to the almshouses. A lot of manual shovelling and carrying of baskets took place. If his father purchased a bullock at Minehead and he couldn't drive it back by road on the hoof, he'd hire a railway truck and have it unloaded at Stogumber and drive it on the hoof to the village. It was killed on site as his father was registered to slaughter the animals. Sometimes they would drive some bullocks by road to Minehead, sell them and return with ten to fifteen sheep. On passing Dunster Lawns they would often see members of the Indian Raj playing polo. They'd brought their horses in by train and they also took over the Metropole Hotel. Joe Sully was one of the local gangers who worked on the permanent way and used the railway shack at Woolston. He worked and walked the line between Williton and Stogumber.

When he left school in 1932, Fred didn't travel so much on the railway, though he did take advantage of the excursion rate to Paddington of 8/6d return. A lifelong Arsenal follower he now and again went to Wembley or Highbury to watch football. He used to spend holidays, two weeks at a time, with his friend Bob Bradshaw, whose father once ran *The Cross Keys* at Taunton. Herbert Chapman, a famous Arsenal manager, was an old family friend and always visited the Bradshaws when holidaying in the West Country and one year they were able to meet him when he gave them each half a crown. That kept Fred in fish and chips for a fortnight. On a later visit to Wembley, having travelled up by train, Fred took his son Robert to see an international football match. They sat just behind the Royal Box and saw Billy Wright with his wife Joy who is one of the Beverley sisters. Robert sneaked off to get Billy's autograph. At first the England captain refused, but Robert kept asking and finally he signed it. Evidently that is still in the family's possession.

He remembers in 1927 seeing the engine *King George V* which had returned from an exhibition in USA. Fred saw it work through Taunton while he happened to be on the station.

When running the shop at Williton in 1939, he sometimes ordered Argentinian meat from Taunton cold storage. It came in on the branch and he would pick it up from the station. However most meat would come in by road, such as frozen New Zealand lamb.

Fred was in the RAF in World War II for four years as an engine fitter and became an NCO. He worked on the Bristol Pegasus engines on the Wellington bombers, which were later replaced by the Hercules engine, which he thought was an excellent engine. He also worked on Halifax bombers and was based with 109 Squadron and later 192 Squadron. At one time he was based in Bedfordshire when a flight of Mosquito aircraft came in from Hatfield. He took the first one in and Sir Geoffrey de Havilland came off the first plane and handed him a box, 'Here you are corporal, see that the lads get this'.

It contained card games, sweets and cigarettes. On another day he met another Mossie, and got the shock of his life when a lovely girl emerged from the cockpit. She had ferried the aircraft all the way from Canada. Fred was mentioned in despatches and has a certificate signed by the then Minister for Air, Harold Macmillan, who went on to become Prime Minister.

Leigh Wood Crossing (*right*) in BR days. After the last train of the day, and by arrangement with the permanent way department, the gatekeepers at Leigh Wood and Roebuck Gate Crossing (*below*) would shut their gates against the running lines. Sheep would then be left to roam between the crossings to keep the grass down along the bank. The PW department were happy, though before the 05.30 newspaper train, the crossing keepers evidently made sure the sheep were clear of the line. One morning the Roebuck Gate Crossing gatekeeper was late up and the first train smashed into the gates. The incident went un-reported. A local carpenter, for a few pints of scrumpy, repaired them and nobody in authority was any the wiser. In the photo below the gates look as though they have been freshly painted. (*both photographs John Pearce collection*)

The stationmaster at Stogumber on the right, with his five children, c.1890s. On the left is an employee, the next two are brothers, both of whom were killed in World War I. The next brother died of natural causes at a young age and the other brother also died in World War I. The little girl is holding her brother's hand. Unfortunately, their names remain unknown, as when the photograph was passed on to us, only the sad details of their young lives were written on the back. Perhaps this was their last picture taken together as a family. (*John Pearce collection*)

Harold Gibbs

Harold was a local lad whose home was in Taunton. After leaving school he applied for, and gained employment as a cleaner on the GWR based at Taunton shed. After a time he graduated to the footplate and became a fireman at Taunton. Harold remembers working on a variety of Prairie Tanks, the 6300 Moguls and the 2251 0-6-0 goods engines. His duty rota set out some weeks of banking at Wellington on the main line to assist trains climbing Whiteball Summit. He also worked over the branches to Barnstaple, Chard, Minehead, Yeovil and sometimes into Ilfracombe on the Southern Region. However, when he saw the Minehead branch on the duty roster he always felt very happy, whether it was working goods or passenger trains.

One of his favourite turns was the first down goods of the day to Minehead, normally worked by a 2251 goods engine, with the load limited by the climb from Bishops Lydeard to Crowcombe. This load could include paraffin, petrol, diesel, coal, coke and food stuffs, all for local consumption. Also the goods train would haul vans containing a large variety of products and sometimes new cars under wraps. On the way to Minehead, wagons were put off

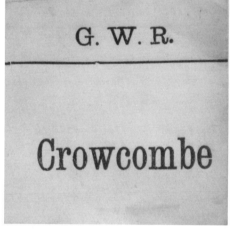

at stations along the line and the goods sheds of Stogumber, Williton, Watchet, Washford and Dunster came into use for the unloading and distribution of the delivered goods. Minehead goods yard was normally reached by 08.15 and once the shunting was finished it was time for breakfast. Now an open cab tender engine would give more room than a tank engine for the cooking of breakfast, done on the firing shovel. It was perfectly healthy as one made the shovel sterile with clean cotton waste, boiling water and intense heat. With the shovel on the fire, a bit of fat was employed and first in were the eggs which once cooked were placed on a tin plate on top of the boiler. Then the bacon, sliced tomatoes and some mushrooms which were often picked from the line side and fried bread. Harold, the driver and guard, who sat on a board in the tender, enjoyed their breakfast in the cab, on their enamel plates, washed

down with a can of tea. The stationmaster being attracted by the smell of cooked bacon would often come to see the breakfast being enjoyed.

Harold worked out of Taunton shed in the early 1950s and remembers how busy Minehead was as a holiday destination with passengers travelling in from London, the Home Counties and the Midlands.

Harold recalls one accident on the footplate of a 2251 class. He worked the 09.30 from Minehead to Taunton with the train formed of a corridor carriage next to the engine and a B set which was two non-corridor carriages permanently coupled together. On this day one of the passengers was Sir Geoffrey Luttrell of Dunster, a former director of the GWR. On arrival at Crowcombe there was a horsebox waiting to be picked up, located in the short siding on the up side at the Stogumber end of the station. The line into the siding was protected by a dummy signal at a catch point controlled from Crowcombe signalbox. Inside the horsebox were two hunters. The passenger train was slowly reversed onto the horsebox and once buffered up, the station porter coupled up the train and horsebox. Unfortunately, the catch point had not been closed from the signalbox; the pair of wheels on the engine side of the rearmost bogie of the last carriage had closed the catch points when the train had come to a complete stop. This caused the dummy signal to come off and give the right away signal. The porter and Harold saw that the signal was off so the right away was given by the porter. Harold passed this on to his driver who gently moved the train forward. Harold looking back was horrified to see the rear carriage and horse box tilted over together and he yelled 'stop' and everything did. On inspection the rear bogie of the last carriage was off the rails; the two horses seemed okay, but were making a noise. In the guard's compartment a woman and baby were screaming. Happily they were not injured. Harold obtained permission from the guard and stationmaster before uncoupling the drawbars between the two B set carriages and blocked up the vacuum pipe with a detonator. With the tail lamp tied in position the train pulled into the up platform and the passengers got into the two front carriages. Sir Geoffrey now made himself known to the footplate crew and informed them of an important appointment he had in London and that he wanted to make his Taunton train connection. Well, they set off for Bishops Lydeard and Norton Fitzwarren and made the Taunton connection just in time. Harold and his driver were both rewarded with 5/- each from Sir Geoffrey. However the carriage supervisor was not best pleased when he saw half the B set missing.

The derailed carriage did not cause an obstruction and to recover it, the next movement was against all regulations. Carriage engineers and permanent way staff joined the train which was then reversed at a reduced speed back to Crowcombe. Here the derailed rolling stock was put back onto the rails and returned to Taunton. An enquiry was held at Newton Abbot resulting in the signalman receiving a registered caution whilst Harold and his driver were awarded official commendations.

He only knew of one fatality on the line and that was at Combe Florey. Some children from a cottage by the main road near the railway line had somehow gone up the railway bank and were playing around the line. A goods train was coming from Crowcombe; the driver thought he saw a red rug or coat between the rails and saw children run away. He blew the whistle, and as he got closer he saw the red bundle move. He braked hard but the engine hit a little girl wearing a red dress and she died instantly. This was a very tragic event for the family; the driver of the engine never got over it.

Another time Harold was going from Stogumber towards Williton when hounds came across the track from a field and were hit by the engine. The result was horrible and a few didn't make it. Fortunately the engine was not going very fast otherwise it could have been a lot worse.

Harold enjoyed his time working out of Taunton shed and on the Minehead branch between 1950 and 1954, and he still pays plenty of visits to the West Somerset Railway.

Driver Stan Blackmore, on the right, and fireman Harold Gibbs are seen here in the cab of class 4575 No.5571 at Fairwater Sidings in 1952. (*Harold Gibbs collection*)

Crowcombe station looks ghostly and desolate in the snow as we look towards Stogumber, except for a lady on the right of the photo. Full marks to the photographer for turning out in the thick snow to take this splendid shot. (*Walter Harris collection*)

Snow on the ground at Crowcombe station makes a lovely atmospheric picture, as a diesel unit arrives from the Minehead direction. The semaphore signalling is still intact and a push bike is leaning against a seat by the waiting room. (*R.J. Sellick/Walter Harris collection*)

Crowcombe station, one of the major passing points on the line, c.1958. Pannier Tank No.3669 was a long-term resident of Taunton shed. It is high summer as the gent on the platform appears to be wearing the latest fashion in shorts. (*Walter Harris collection*)

Class 6100 No.6157 eases into Crowcombe with a four-coach passenger train for Taunton. There appears to be plenty of smoke and steam to spare. (*Walter Harris collection*)

A down six-coach passenger train hauled by No.5525 nears the end of the long climb from Bishops Lydeard into Crowcombe. Once the train leaves, the fireman can ease up as the train heads down towards Williton. This could be the summer of 1958 as this engine arrived on the stock of Taunton shed in June 1958. (*Walter Harris collection*)

Michael Hodge

My first trip on the Taunton to Minehead line was on 6 May 1964. Having moved from Weston-super-Mare to Cannington on 4 May, we thought we would like to have an afternoon off. The Minehead branch was a line on which I had never travelled and it had been mentioned as a likely candidate for closure in the Beeching report of 1 March 1963. On the day we travelled we went from Bridgwater, changing at Taunton and on to Minehead. We subsequently used the line quite often but normally joined the train at Crowcombe, as it was then called, as this station was a convenient 10-mile delightful climb over the Quantock Hills. On the first trip little did I realise that within seven years I would actually be working as a volunteer on the line and four years later, in 1975, appointed joint stationmaster with Walter Harris at what is now called Crowcombe Heathfield. We have many happy memories and looking back it is obvious that when closure was actually proposed in 1968, the figures quoted were massaged to make the case for financial justification of the closure. Furthermore, no effort was made to promote the use of the line.

The opening of Butlin's holiday camp in the mid-sixties did bring very useful revenue in the holiday season. On summer Saturdays six-car sets were packed to the doors. I recall one event in particular which must have been repeated countless times on other occasions. In August 1968 just before closure was announced, an illustration of lack of revenue protection occurred as by this time, there were no ticket-issuing facilities between Bishops Lydeard and Minehead. We bought a train ticket. When the train left Watchet, it was full to overflowing. I recall that virtually all the passengers joining from the latter stations onwards had paid no fare. I raised the matter with British Railways who informed me that they could not afford to collect fares from those coming off the trains at Minehead except on a summer Saturday.

Another recollection is the Great Western Society of Taunton running a special on the last day of operations by BR on 2 January 1971. It was called 'The Last Daylight Train' and was exceedingly well patronised.

(*right*) Preservation has begun as a team of enthusiasts move into Barry scrap yard in 1970. From left to right: Chris Young, unknown, Tony Bulmore, Ray Lee and, yes, that is John Pearce. The lads are carrying coupling rods from class 4575 No.5539 for spares for a 4500 rebuild. (*John Pearce collection*)

An old postcard showing Bishops Lydeard in Edwardian times. As usual, the staff knew their picture was being taken. Advertisements and notices adorn the station building and the whole station has an aura of tidiness about it. (*West Somerset Steam Railway Trust collection*)

John Harris

I joined the Western Region on 9 April 1956 and was employed as a porter on Taunton station. Part of my duties was looking after passengers and making sure the parcels and luggage were taken care of. Milk in churns from the local dairies and parcels came off the Minehead branch. Colleagues I recall from those days included porter Eddie Thompson, coach shunter Roy Wadham, chief inspector Bill Lee and inspector Clarence Hawkes who had given me my job. I filled a vacancy later for a parcels porter; for this I earned an extra 1/- a day and later inspector Lee passed me out for shunting at Taunton. You had to get under the coaches and hook them up which was hard work. I also carried out goods shunting as well, using the long shunting pole which had a metal hook on the end.

When I was made redundant as a passenger shunter, I was moved to a crossing west of Taunton in the Exeter direction. For five years I also worked on the coaling plant at Taunton, and when the coaling plant was closed I was automatically transferred to a shunter's job. Sometimes I rode on the footplate when the job required it. Then I moved onto the Minehead branch, working at Leigh Wood Crossing which was situated between Crowcombe and Stogumber.

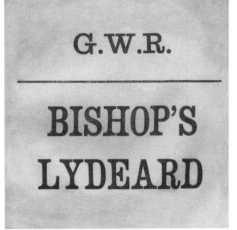

In the 1950s the branch was very busy with both goods and passenger traffic. I would travel down on the engine and the driver would stop to let me off. I would open the gates and the train would be back down the branch. One day at 06.30 I drove my car to Leigh Wood Crossing in the snow. Driving uphill near Crowcombe on an S bend, I found Dunster signalman Dennis Davey off the road. So we stopped the first train from Bishops Lydeard at Leigh Wood and Dennis got on board. We phoned Blue Anchor signalbox and got Harold Brue to let the train run through to Dunster without a token, and to inform Mrs. Baker at Sea Lane Crossing. How they eventually worked this all out I don't know.

At the crossing I had very little to do; mind you, I did enjoy chats with the local people. The only highlight was chasing cows off the line. My opposite number at the crossing was George Warren, a good mate. Summer Saturdays would be a 12-hour shift at the crossing or,

when needed, I would go to Minehead to do some shunting. I was at Leigh Woods Crossing until it closed.

I remember one shunter who would bring his food to work, often mouldy bread with mouldy cheese, and it would make me feel sick. Francis (Frankie) Fyffe was another shunter who lived at Trull, near Taunton. Well, one day, he shunted a passenger train at Taunton, he cut the engine off, ran it round, but only coupled the brake pipes up and forgot the coupling. When crossing over the track, the pipes stretched and a coach was derailed. Frankie got away with it, as the driver felt a bump when he crossed over and thought the coupling must have jumped off the hook. However the down relief, up main and down main lines were blocked and only the up relief line could be used until the blockage was removed.

One day a first-class coach came down from Bristol on the back of the 18.35 from Neyland; we shunted it over to No.9 bay. I told Roy Wadham what had been done. 'Stupid bugger' he said, 'that should have stayed on that set as it was positioned for the Queen to travel on'.

I remember Bertram Mills Circus being unloaded at Taunton. It was shunted into the up dock and the elephants walked up the street and around the town to advertise the circus.

During one hard winter I operated the steam lances connected to the front of the steam engines, to blast the snow and ice out of the points, so the signalmen could operate them and we could run trains. More than once I manned the barriers at Silk Mills Crossing during single line working, where we would open a little box, wherein a lever was used to operate the barrier when the signalman told us a train was leaving Taunton. I do recall a couple of near misses with the barrier.

At Crowcombe Ron Moore was the signalman and he would climb up the signal ladders to change the lamps or clean the lamp spectacles. Other staff I remember were Sammy Jacques who was a signalman at Dunster and Harold Brue who worked in Blue Anchor box. The third step was always loose there. I knew Stan Taylor on the permanent way; he lived at Williton. I spent 42 years and 10 months working on the railway.

A photograph of Bishops Lydeard showing the stationmaster's house on the left and on the right the signalbox. Both buildings are in use today. The loco is BR 2-6-2T No.82044 on what looks like a through train. It has the road and is ready to go. (*Walter Harris collection*)

D6334 is about to stop at Bishops Lydeard with the 14.30 from Minehead to Taunton passenger train in August 1965. (*Owen Mogg/Peter Triggs collection*)

(*right*) Porter Derrick Lock stands by the railway's Austin goods lorry at Bishops Lydeard station, c.1950s. Derrick later went on to be a relief signalman on the branch. (*Peter Lock*)

(*left*) Based at Taunton station, lorry driver Dennis Foyle is seen here in his cab at Bishops Lydeard, after delivering goods to the station. (Peter Lock)

(*right*) Looking out of the cab is driver Roy Cross complete with beret. Roy gave over 49 years' service to the railway. How many of us will work for one company for that length of time? (*Melvyn Baker collection*)

(*left*) Bishops Lydeard and Crowcombe stationmaster Frank Pardoe poses for the camera on the platform at Lydeard. On the right is the station house where he lived in the 1950s. (*Peter Lock*)

(*right*) Lad porter Peter Lock (brother of Derrick) on his trusty bike at his home station of Bishops Lydeard. (*Peter Lock collection*)

(*left*) Passengers, from left to right, are Lilian Lock, Nellie Pomroy and Arthur Pomroy at Bishops Lydeard station, awaiting a train for a trip to Minehead in the 1950s. (*Peter Lock*)

On a fine summer's day the view from the road bridge at Bishops Lydeard station is shown looking towards Taunton, c.1950s. The signalbox can be seen in the distance. (*R. Carpenter collection*)

With plenty of steam to spare class 5700 No.9732 is seen at Norton Fitzwarren station. The shed code at the bottom of the smokebox door helps date the picture, as 71H was coded Yeovil Pen Mill from 23 February 1958. No.9732 was transferred away when the shed closed on 5 January 1959. (*John Pearce collection*)

(*above*) Seen here at Norton Fitzwarren in 1963 is BR Standard No.82008 on a very short goods from the Barnstaple branch. On the right of the photograph is the Railway Hotel. (*Owen Mogg/Peter Triggs collection*)

(*right*) Joe and Lilian Backham looking very smart on the day of their retirement from the Railway Hotel at Norton Fitzwarren in the late 1950s. How many pints had they served to thirsty railwaymen over the years? Their children Colleen, Josephine and Tina were known as The Railway Children because of the amount of waving they gave to footplate crews and passengers. In fact Colleen married a railwayman.(*Colleen Baker collection*)

Melvyn Baker

From the age of five, railways have been the great love of my life, especially the GWR. As a boy the only places to be for the best views of trains were Railway Street and Forty Steps in Taunton. With all my family on the railway it was too much to resist and I became a cleaner at Taunton. I duly went to Swindon for my medical where I was called into the doctor's room. The first instruction was, 'fill this can behind the curtain'. It looked like a normal tea can, but he did not want tea.

I started work as a cleaner in August 1961; I was 15 years old. I was only cleaning for 10 months, then became a passed cleaner which allowed me to go firing when there was a shortage of men. Other colleagues there at that time were cleaners Roy Yandall, (who walked from Bagborough in the snow of 1963 not to miss a day's work), Dave Webber, chargemen Ned Widgery and Tommy Sampson. My first firing turn I recall, was on Saturday 5 May which was Cup Final day. I booked on at 13.30 and walked to Fairwater Yard to relieve the early turn men. Saturday afternoon was always quiet in the yards, we made a few shunts then went into the shunter's cabin to listen to the match. I returned to the engine every half-hour to check the fire and water level in the boiler. A few more shunts would be made in the evening before taking the engine to shed.

A pastime for young firemen and shunters at Fairwater Yard on summer evenings was to creep down behind the hedges and frighten the courting couples who used the fields at the back of the yard. Another job would be the 02.00 engine prep; this was one of the hardest turns at Taunton. After booking on you would draw oil from the stores and pinch tools from other engines. As the steam engines were being phased out, tools were in short supply. The driver would oil round while the fireman made up the fire. The following engines would be prepared: the 04.20 Woodford Halse, normally a 28xx – we had two at Taunton, 2822 and 2882; the 05.05 Tiverton goods, normally a 41xx large Prairie Tank; 06.20 Yeovil goods which was always a Pannier Tank; the 08.05

G.W.R.

Taunton

Barnstaple passenger, a 63xx Mogul; and the last engine on that turn, the 09.45 Yeovil passenger with a 45xx.

I do remember going down the branch to Watchet in 1962. One of the last goods to come out of Watchet Docks was esparto grass, a coarse brown material in large bales from Africa. The grass was very heavy as four bales would fill a 13ft 5in plank, open truck. The motive power was always a Pannier Tank which had an axle loading light enough to enter Watchet Docks. The grass train workings were in the spare link, as they operated as required by the docking of the ship. You would book on at 06.00 and prepare your engine.

One of the many Pannier Tanks based at Taunton was No.8783, a very strong little engine. The paintwork had faded and you could plainly see GWR on the tank sides, 14 years after nationalisation. I don't think it ever received the early or late British Railways crest. After preparing your engine for which you were allowed 45 minutes, you proceeded to west yard to collect your train of empty 13-ton opens, plus the brakevan and guard, who would also be the shunter when we got to Watchet. Of course the most important thing before going off shed was to make a can of tea. This was the block train working, long before British Railways introduced them as a new concept.

After coupling up to your train you proceeded to Watchet; the guard would unlock the points enabling you to reverse the train down into the dock area. The points would then be reset so the branch could operate without any interference from us. After several hours of shunting we would stop for breakfast, normally joining the guard in his van which was warmed up by the pot belly stove, a standard fitting in all guards vans. This was very welcome in the winter and shielded us from the bitter winds of the Bristol Channel.

All shunting completed, it would be time to build up the fire for the hard slog back up the bank to Crowcombe. If you had Welsh steam coal, which GWR engines were designed to burn with their large fireboxes, the job would be easy. The large lumps could be fed into the firebox by hand and it would burn slowly until you got to Williton. Then with the exhaust from the smoke box it would draw into a mass of fire; it looked like a box of cauliflowers. You could sit down going up the bank, with just a few shovelfuls around the box and put the injector on, but if you had a bunker of ovoids (man-made coal dust mixed with a tar compound) it would burn very quickly, then settle on the fire bars with a blue flame, clinkering up the fire, which meant no heat and no steam. With this type of coal you could have a bad trip and on occasions you had to stop at Stogumber for a blow up and to fill the boiler.

Ready to go, we would run round our train, the guard would get permission from Williton signalbox to unlock the points and propel our train onto the branch. Then forward to Williton to take water, change the staff, then up the bank to Crowcombe, watching the steam gauge all the time, hoping you would make it, firing little and often and keeping the boiler topped up. A great deal depended on your driver. If I had my regular mate, Roy Cross, who had just become a driver after firing for 20 years, he would be very considerate with the steam available, as would others who had just been made up to drivers like Des Alderton, Ern Dingle, Fred Mace and Lionel Cox. If you were unlucky you could be put with one of the older drivers who had been taken off the main line for medical reasons. Jack Wilson's idea of driving was to open the regulator full and shut it when you reached a station, or driver Sleepy Holloway who would get the

train on the move then close his eyes leaning on the reverser, but never fail to wake up when approaching a station.

Successfully reaching Crowcombe, change the staff and ease the train away down the bank to Bishops Lydeard, ensuring you kept the speed down to prevent a runaway. You would give the staff up at Lydeard and then you were on double track to Norton Fitzwarren where you joined the main line. On the relief to Silk Mills, crossing over to gain access to Fairwater Yard, we would leave our train and go to shed. The pilot would shunt the guards van to the other end of the train ready for another engine to come off shed and take the train to Silverton Paper Mills, normally a Hall/Grange type tender engine.

The 82xxx class were the only Standards we had at Taunton, all in green livery except 82008 and 82044 which were BR black. This was the only class of engine at our shed that was fitted with a speedometer, a great novelty at times. You could get the speedo past the 80mph mark bunker first, with coal dust everywhere, but a great ride until you hit the Creech Junction crossover that went to the Chard branch, then she would buck and jump and you thought you were off the rails. If you were on time you would overtake a down North of England to Plymouth diesel-hauled express; oh, the look on the passengers' and crew's faces.

No.82008 working a four-coach train into Taunton. It's 19 October 1963 and the reason for the large gathering of trainspotters at the platform is that No. 4472 *Flying Scotsman* was due shortly. Note the policeman on the right-hand side of the platform, the short haircuts, bearing in mind it was the start of the swinging sixties, and the sparse scattering of camera equipment. (*Peter Triggs*)

Steam at Taunton was enjoying an Indian summer. I was in the Chard and Yeovil link and was lucky to work the last passenger train on the branch, stopping at all stations in September 1962. We were on Pannier Tank No. 8783 with driver Roy Anstice.

This brings back a memory I have on the Chard Mail, my very first passenger firing turn at the tender age of 16, with an old driver Reg Travers. I was very nervous, but the job was easy enough. We always arrived in Taunton on the down main platform 5, normally before 22.16. That first night came as rather a shock as we stopped, Reg jumped down onto the track and ran like a young buck across the down relief, leapt up on to the platform and at 64 years of age that was some doing. As he disappeared he shouted back, 'see you in the shed'; what do I do now? The signal came off, then the shunter appeared, he could see how young I was. I said 'the driver won't be long', but he replied, 'you won't see him for a bit; he has gone down *The Wheeltappers* for a couple of pints before they close, that's why this train is always early. It's your job to drive the train over to the coach sidings, then I will uncouple you, then you take the engine to shed; he will see you there but you don't tell anyone'. Nobody in those days would get their mate into trouble.

In September 1962 we were on the early morning passenger train and had the engineers on board who got off at Chard Central. I asked them what they had come to do. 'We have to fit all new lavatory cisterns in the toilets'. I commented that the station closed for good the next night. 'That's nothing to do with us', they said.

One memorable trip I had on the Barnstaple branch was on Pannier Tank No. 9663. It had just returned from an overhaul at Swindon. Everything was fine until we left East Anstey. Going down the bank towards South Molton my driver Roy Cross closed the regulator, but to our amazement we kept steaming along. The regulator appeared closed, but it wasn't closing the steam valve to the cylinders. We made several further attempts but to no avail. We had the steam brake and the hand brake on, we blew the emergency whistle for the guard to put his brake on. I started to throw the fire out, but as the steam pressure dropped so did the effectiveness of the steam brake. On reaching the platform at South Molton, we were now down to a crawl, but still could not stop her. We both jumped off and she went on

to hit the stop blocks. Luckily there was no damage to the train and she was still puffing away whilst standing there. We threw the fire out and reported to control that we had a problem. We left her there and caught the passenger train home and filled out the many forms. We knew it could have been a very serious accident. The next day 9663 was towed back to Taunton for an examination. We had to face an enquiry which could have led to disciplinary action if it was found human error was to blame, which was never the case. It was found that the regulator rod that passes through the boiler had been replaced during the overhaul at Swindon and had a hairline crack in it which completely broke when the regulator was closed on leaving East Anstey.

One peaceful morning parked in number 9 bay with No.4932, *Hatherton Hall*, I was enjoying a can of tea and reading the paper with my regular mate Roy Cross. The platform inspector came up to us to say the up Torbay Express was in trouble and had asked for assistance to Paddington (my moment of glory to fire steam to the big city), but then we were told we would be relieved at Westbury. After about 30 minutes the signal came off for us to go over on to the up main and wait for the train to arrive on platform 6. We backed down onto the train and I coupled up while Roy put a few more shovelfuls around. A whistle from the guard and we were off, only 16 years old and firing the Torbay Express, what all schoolboys' dreams are made of. We had 12 coaches and a sick Warship diesel to get to Paddington on time with this old rundown steam engine with a cracked frame, but Mr. Collett made his engines to last. We went up Brewham Bank down into Westbury for relief, but not this day. The inspector came up to us and said: 'sorry boys, no relief, do you know the road to Reading?' My mate Roy knew the road to Paddington, so off we went up over Savernake, my back now beginning to ache. I am thinking to myself this is a lot different than the Minehead branch, on into Reading for the relief. I was a little disappointed that we were not going all the way to London, a childhood ambition, but to get this far was a great experience.

On arrival at Reading I looked up the platform for our relief but no one was in sight. I cleaned up the footplate ready for a quick change over, looked back up the platform, still no sign of the relief. The guard blew his whistle, the RA sign came up on the end of the platform and off we went, next stop Paddington. We went through Sonning Cutting along Brunel's straight level track, a few more shovelfuls, little and often and enjoy the thrill. The old girl was now doing 90 mph; soon we were slowing down and approaching the suburbs. I was amazed there were so many signals, then into the great glass Cathedral that is Paddington. One of the great moments of my life that I will never forget.

On another turn I booked on at 14.15 on 28 May 1963 for the Wellington goods with driver R. Grundy, which was cancelled. Instead we were told to work a special of basic slag ex Hallens Marsh, Avonmouth to Hackney Yard, Newton Abbot. We walked to the east yard and relieved a Bristol crew on 6816 *Frankton Grange*, a favourite class of engine among footplate staff. After exchanging the usual footplate information we went down the goods loop past West Yard out onto the down main. The Bristol fireman had left a good fire which was a blessing with such a heavy

16-year-old fireman Melvyn Baker leans out of the cab of a Mogul No.7304. The highlight of his railway career was firing an express to Paddington. How many of us wished that we had done that? (*Melvyn Baker collection*)

train, and we were then on to Wellington. We were then put into the platform road to let the Cornish Riviera pass, diesel-hauled as most passenger trains now were. The banker came on the rear; the 61xx class had now given way to the D7xxx Hymek. In the past, if a tender engine was on banking duties and the driver had an inexperienced fireman, he would play a little joke on him. On entering the tunnel he would walk around the front of the engine and look in through the spectacle glass on the fireman's side, giving the poor lad the shock of his life.

Away we went in fine style. These Granges could certainly pull, up Whiteball, into the tunnel and an easy ride down to Exeter through the middle road then out along the seawall. On a lovely sunny afternoon, watching the holiday makers enjoying themselves on the beach, is something I will never forget. Some turned to look at us, as it was now rare to see a steam engine west of Taunton, as there were no servicing facilities on the Western Region in Devon or Cornwall. We left our train in Hackney Yard, went into the Newton Abbot diesel depot and turned on the turntable. We then took on water and came back light engine to Taunton. This had been a perfect day and I was sorry it was about to end.

Next month I was sent with a few other firemen to Laira, Plymouth, so that we could learn how to operate the steam heating boilers that were fitted to the hydraulic diesels. It was a week's course and very enjoyable; we were accommodated in the drivers' hostel which used to be made available for double home crews, long since discontinued by British Railways.

On the Friday afternoon at the end of the course we caught the train back to Taunton, full of hope for the future, but enclosed with our pay packets were our redundancy notices. It was a sad end to a very short but enjoyable career.

(*left*) Memories of happy summer Saturdays train-spotting at Taunton station in 1959. The well-known Derek Arnold is in the centre with one of the enthusiasts inspecting all his pens. Does anybody recognise themselves? (*Peter Triggs*)

(*right*) How many years service have they between them, as the parcels department line up in front of a BR parcels lorry at Taunton station in the 1960s? From left to right: Peter Lock, Edgar Tratt, Ted Gardner, Bernard Suter, Marcia ?, Sid Sampson, Paddy Fletcher, Eric ?, Merv Eggbeer and Bert Waygood. (*Peter Lock collection*) (*right*) Porter John Harris doing a fine job of painting the white line on the platform at Taunton station. (*John Harris collection*)

(*below*) A group picture of staff taken at Taunton station. From left to right: John Harris (shunter), Lionel Cox (driver), Bob Thomas (driver), Wally Pipe (inspector), Ern Dingle (driver) and Eric Jeanes (signalman). (*John Harris collection*)

(*left*) Driver Reg Penny, on the left, with another driver Lionel Cox, on the Minehead to Paddington train at Taunton with No.4087 *Cardigan Castle*. This was Reg's last day before retirement and his old mate Lionel agreed to be his fireman on his final trip. (*Melvyn Baker collection*)

(*below*) Signalman Derrick Lock in charge of the busy signalbox at Silk Mills, which was just over 160 miles from Paddington and about 24 miles from Minehead. (*Peter Lock*)

130

No.6019 *King Henry V* is at the head of a Minehead to Paddington train, c.1961. In GWR and WR days this class of 30 engines was banned from running on many lines including the Minehead branch. How times have changed as one of the survivors, 6024 *King Edward I*, has since worked on the WSR. (*Peter Triggs*)

On a lovely sunny day on 6 April 1962 class 5100 No.4103 is on its way to the seaside town of Minehead with a four-coach passenger train. (*John Pearce collection*)

This is quite a rare sight of the doyen of the class 4700 2-8-0 on a passenger train at Taunton in 1960, seen here working a Paddington to Kingswear train. They were introduced by Churchward in 1919 as a mixed traffic design. There were nine of the class numbered 4700-4708. (*John Pearce collection*)

A Barnstaple-bound train awaits departure from Taunton in 1964 behind BR class 3 No.82030, an engine that also worked the Minehead branch. (*John Pearce collection*)

Taunton in GW days with a double-headed train from Paddington that would work on to Minehead. The leading locomotive is a Bulldog No.3375 *Sir Watkin Wynn* while the second engine is a GWR 2-6-2T. (*John Pearce collection*)

D1035 *Western Yeoman* shunting in platform 6 at Taunton, c.1962. Melvyn Baker, the second man can be seen looking back towards the carriages. (*Melvyn Baker collection*)

(*above*) The Torbay Express at Taunton with Warship class No.D843 *Sharpshooter* in charge. (*Melvyn Baker collection*)

(*below*) A Minehead-bound DMU about to pick up the single line token for the first section of the branch from Silk Mills signal-man John Macdonald, on 1 January 1971. In the DMU are driver Fred Blew and second man Walter Caddick. (*John Cornelius*)

The Last Trains on the Minehead Tiddler

One of the last trains that went from Taunton to Minehead on Saturday 2 January 1971 was run by the Great Western Society, South West Group, Taunton branch. The train left Taunton at 15.30 and returned at 17.20; the fare was £1. The driver of the DMU was Ken Cridland. The last train left Taunton at 21.40 which was the return part of the Minehead Round Table's Special and the 21.10 service train.

There was a delay of 90 minutes as someone had pulled the communication cord at Williton. The very last service train left Minehead at 23.40 and arrived at Taunton at 00.40 on the Sunday. We have put together a collection of photographs and a memory from a driver, of the day's events, where many local people said a sad farewell to the Minehead Tiddler, as it was affectionately known.

Ern Dingle

The final curtain – an era draws to a close

There was no inkling of what was to follow on that fateful day in January 1971; it had started just like any other, signing on and reading the daily Ops notices as usual. I was booked to take a late afternoon six-coach empty coaching stock train down the branch to form what was to be the last passenger service out of Minehead. After signing on at 17.00 and carrying out my normal preparation work, I waited for the 'road' and then duly set off on my way. It had been an uneventful journey down, like many others before it, but nothing had prepared me for what I was to see at Minehead. After leaving Dunster, running across the Marshes and then on down along the final straight, I soon became aware of more bodies on the platform than I had seen there before; the closer I got, the more there seemed to be; I was totally unprepared for what was to happen next; as I eased the throttle back and started to draw in to the main platform, the Band struck up and even started to drown out the noise of the running engines. So much noise and so many people – if only, I thought, such numbers had been around in the past to support and ride the Branch on a regular basis, then this fateful day may never have been. Much pomp and ceremony, together with speeches from the assembled dignitaries ensued before the allotted departure time of 20.25. Special 'Last Train' tickets had been produced for the journey; these were priced at 20 shillings for the full return journey from Minehead to Taunton and back, with the train calling at all the stations along the line. I was given one of these commemorative mounted tickets together with a booklet highlighting the history of the Line.

It was an emotive farewell to Minehead with cameras clicking everywhere as we slowly pulled away. I had driven this Branch many times before but this was to be a journey unlike any other; the Band was aboard and played throughout; I recall there being cameras everywhere as we made our journey up the line, with warm but tearful welcomes awaiting at each of the stops on the way up to Taunton. I brought us to rest in our usual place in the Bay at Taunton and reflected on what might have been if only the line had been so well supported in the past; this was the end of an era – one that I had never thought would come. I and many of my colleagues from Taunton had been up and down the line on so many occasions, that we regarded the Branch as part of a daily life that would go on for ever; although we had seen its effects elsewhere, we had not reckoned on the reality of the 'Beeching' axe on this part of our lives. As I signed off for the day, it was with more than a little tear that I reflected that I would no longer see the changing effect of the seasons on the countryside or the varying wildlife up and down the line; nor would I see again the regular commuters and the schoolchildren I had come to recognise as they went about their daily business. No longer would I see the eagerness and excitement on the faces of the holiday children anxious to get to their seaside homes; but perhaps most of all, I realised I was going to miss all my friends and colleagues on the stations and in the signalboxes that I had come to know over the years – what, I wondered, was the future to hold for us all? After such an emotive journey, I was grateful that I had not been booked to take the returning service down to Minehead; that fell to one of my colleagues, Dougie Sampson, who also had the final indignity of bringing the 'ghostly' empties back to Taunton, leaving Minehead finally bereft of a passenger service.

These are the recollections of Ern Dingle, a local man based at Taunton shed until it closed and who then transferred to Exeter, until he finally retired in December 1989, after 47 years on the railway.

(*above*) This is the last official through train into Watchet on 2 January 1971. Dr. Beeching has a lot to answer for. (*David Frier*)

(*right*) With the passing of the last train into Watchet, the Mayor, members of the council and local people are seen at the station. People in the photo include Wally West, Jim Chilcott, David Cornelius, Mrs. Southern, Norman Farmer, Simon Farmer, Eileen Woods, Mrs. West & Henry Chibbett. (*David Frier*)

(*left*) The Minehead brass band, with bandmaster Derek Fairchild holding the baton, are entertaining the crowds of local people who are out in force for the last trains in and out of Minehead. (*L.T. Blackmore/Trevor Martin collection*)

(*below*) Two attractive programme sellers welcome the special Great Western Society train into Minehead. We would certainly buy a programme from them. (*L.T. Blackmore/ Trevor Martin collection*)

(*below*) The banner of the Great Western Society says it all. But not all is lost. The Phoenix has risen again with the West Somerset Railway. (*L.T. Blackmore/Trevor Martin collection*)

(*right*) The banner of the Great Western Society is hung with pride on the DMU on the last day. (*L.T. Blackmore/Trevor Martin collection*)

(*below*) A last day special on the Minehead branch, with a DMU hired by the Great Western Society, Taunton branch, to run the length of the branch on 2 January 1971. The train is seen at Stogumber with British Transport policeman Bob Reid keeping an eye on the activities. (*John Cornelius*)

Index

Alderton, Des 125
Aldridge, Christine 28
Amies, Gertrude 71
Amies, Stan 67,70,84,85
Anstice, Roy 126
Arnold, Alan 21
Arnold, Derek 128
Atkins, Alison 42
Aylesbury, Clarence 21

Backham, Colleen 123
Backham, Joe 123
Backham, Josephine 123
Backham, Lilian 123
Backham, Tina 123
Baker, Melvyn 37,51,124-127,136
Baker, Mrs 115
Bale, Hilda 78
Bale, Josephine 78
Bartlett, Ada 15
Bedford, June 64
Bedford, Stan 64-65
Beel, Richard 32-34
Bending, Reg 13
Berryman, Mervyn 10,11,20
Binding, Jack 81
Binding, Robert 82
Bishop, Harry 53
Bissell, Frank 94
Blackmore, Stan 107
Blew, Fred 137
Bradshaw, Bob 102
Bradshaw (née Reed), Vera 14-17
Brambell, Wilfrid 42,43
Brewer, Mrs 30
Brooks, George 64
Brue, Harold 115
Bulmore, Tony 113
Burdge, Barbara 64-65

Caddick, Walter 137
Case, Arthur 20,23
Case, Norman 21
Case, Sam 15,20,21,23,95,100
Chapman, Herbert 102
Chibbett, Henry 139
Chidgey, Fred 15,16,100

Chilcott, Jim 139
Clare, Harry 34
Clarke, Arthur C. 102
Clavey, Jack 71
Cockrem, John 50-51
Cole, Reg 95
Cole, Sid 46,47
Cole, Sue 44
Coles, Fred 15,20,21
Connett, Mr 20
Cornelius, David 139
Cornish, Reg 69
Cornish, Ron 70,94,99
Cornish, Sam 10,15,20,21
Cox, Lionel 125,129,130
Crawford, Violet 14-17
Cridland, Ken 84,138
Crocker, John 54
Crockford, Ernie 20,21,35
Cross, Alfie 95
Cross, Roy 39,118,125-127

Davey, Dennis 94,115
Davis, Jack 10,12,15,16,20
Davis, Ron 20
Day, Jim 94
Dean, Stan 35
Denny, Mr 21
Dilley, William 92
Dingle, Ern 125,129,138
Dinwiddy, Dan 15
Doble, Jimmy 17,21
Dudridge, Percy 102
Dunscombe, Stan 20,23

Earl, Winnie 14-17
Eggbeer, Merv 128

Fairchild, Derek 140
Farmer, Norman 139
Farmer, Simon 139
Fitzgerald, Harry 21
Fletcher, Paddy 128
Floyd, Carrier 34
Floyd, Doris 32,34
Floyd, Will 32,34
Forsyth, John 94

Foyle, Dennis 118
Fullard, Charlie 20
Fyffe, Francis 115

Gardner, Ted 128
Gibbs, Harold 106-107
Goostrey, Jack 85
Gould (*née* Hunt), Margaret 44-46
Grady, Ian 50
Greenslade, Bill 14,50
Grundy, R. 127

Hall (*née* Swainsbury), Judy 28,58
Harris, John 115,129
Harris, Percy 10,11,20
Harris, Walter 113
Harrison, George 43
Hartnell, Des 13
Hawkes, Clarence 92,94,115
Haynes, Mike 60
Heard, Hetty 14-17
Hensley, Bob 86,95,100
Hewart, James 35
Heywood, Ron 12,20-21
Hill, Ken 92-94
Hill, Russell 92,93
Hobbs, Percy 15,20,21,47
Hobbs, Roy 14,44,47
Hodge, Michael 113
Holloway, Sleepy 125
Horn, Harry 79,86,92,93,97,98
Howe, Percy 13,20,35
Hudson, Mr 20
Hunt, Eleanor 44-46,47
Hunt, Jim 44-46,47
Hunt, Joe 80,85
Hutchings, Fred 100-103
Hutchins, Mr 100

Jacques, Sam 71,94,115
Jeanes, Eric 129
Jones, Richard 65

Kemp, Tommy 20,47
Kidson, Leon 70,94,97-99
Kirkland, Harry 68
Knight, William 66,78,80

Lake, Mr 50
Lee, Bill 115

Lee, Joe 85
Lee, Ray 113
Lennon, John 42,43
Littlefield, Alfie 21,35
Lock, Derrick 118,130
Lock, Lilian 119
Lock, Peter 119,128
Lockwood, Peter 26
Loyd, Harry 50
Luttrell, Sir Geoffrey 106-7
Luxton, George 14,20,21

Macdonald, John 137
Mace, Fred 125
Mandley, Bill 50
Manning, Ralph 92
Marley, Miss 34
Martin, Charlie 86,95
Martin, Edward 86
Martin, Phyllis 86
Martin, Steve 37
Martin, Trevor 86-87
May, Ron 21,46,92
McCartney, Paul 42,43
Meade, Gordon 12,21
Millar, Gilbert 95
Mogg, Louie 47
Moody, Mr 14
Moore, Mr 99
Moore, Ron 115
Morris, Mr 20

Neville, Jim 20
Norman, May 67
Page, Grahame 28

Palk, Len 20
Palmer, Alfie 95
Palmer, Chris 94,99
Palmer, Mike 63
Pardoe, Frank 119
Payne, Harry 93
Payne, Henry 71
Pearce, John 113
Peel, Tommy 82
Penny, Norman 93
Penny, Reg 130
Phillips, Tom 13
Phippen, Harry 21
Pinkham, Charlie 37

Pipe, Wally 129
Pitman, Roy 63
Pomroy, Arthur 119
Pomroy, Nellie 119
Pomroy, Olive 31
Porton, Alan 40
Potter, Stan 50,107

Quinton, Miss 34

Rawlings, Kate 58
Redfern, Johnny 21
Reeder, George 66
Reeder, Jack 66-69,71
Reid, Bob 141
Richie, Gordon 68
Robjohn, Les 102
Robjohn, Peter 102
Rogers, Arthur 99
Roll, Farmer 34
Rose, Ernest 13,20,21

Sampson, Dougie 138
Sampson, Sid 128
Sampson, Tommy 124
Sheppard, Chris 78-79
Short, Frank 94
Smallridge, Charles 14,15,16,20
Smith, George 92,93,94
Snell, Norman 47
Southern, Mrs 139
Sparks, Harry 15,16,20
Spencer, Donald 11,13
Stagg, Graham 66
Starr, Ringo 42,43
Stenner, Josh 34
Stevens, Elizabeth 37
Stevens, Ena 15,37
Stewart, Tom 10,14,15,16,20,21
Stone, Cecil 69
Storey, Bill 21
Strong, Robin 21
Sully, Arthur 77,80
Sully, Joe 102
Suter, Bernard 128
Swainsbury, Albert 28
Symonds, Harry 86-87

Taylor, Albert 50
Taylor, Stan 115

Thomas, Bob 129
Thompson, Eddie 115
Thyer, Walter 84
Tratt, Edgar 128
Travers, Reg 126
Tudball, Tom 70

Wadham, Roy 115
Warr, Charlie 95
Warren, George 115
Waygood, Bert 128
Webber, Dave 124
West, Mrs 139
West, Wally 139
White, Stan 53
White, Tom 102
Widden, Will 30
Widgery, Ned 124
Williams, Percy 69
Williams, Tony 50
Wilson, Jack 125
Woods, Eileen 139
Woolford, David 10-12

Yandall, Roy 124
Young, Chris 113